NATIONAL STRATEGY FOR
HOMELAND SECURITY

HOMELAND SECURITY COUNCIL
OCTOBER 2007

My fellow Americans,

More than 6 years after the attacks of September 11, 2001, we remain at war with adversaries who are committed to destroying our people, our freedom, and our way of life. In the midst of this conflict, our Nation also has endured one of the worst natural disasters in our history, Hurricane Katrina. As we face the dual challenges of preventing terrorist attacks in the Homeland and strengthening our Nation's preparedness for both natural and man-made disasters, our most solemn duty is to protect the American people. The *National Strategy for Homeland Security* serves as our guide to leverage America's talents and resources to meet this obligation.

Despite grave challenges, we also have seen great accomplishments. Working with our partners and allies, we have broken up terrorist cells, disrupted attacks, and saved American lives. Although our enemies have not been idle, they have not succeeded in launching another attack on our soil in over 6 years due to the bravery and diligence of many.

Just as our vision of homeland security has evolved as we have made progress in the War on Terror, we also have learned from the tragedy of Hurricane Katrina. We witnessed countless acts of courage and kindness in the aftermath of that storm, but I, like most Americans, was not satisfied with the Federal response. We have applied the lessons of Katrina to this *Strategy* to make sure that America is safer, stronger, and better prepared.

To best protect the American people, homeland security must be a responsibility shared across our entire Nation. As we further develop a national culture of preparedness, our local, Tribal, State, and Federal governments, faith-based and community organizations, and businesses must be partners in securing the Homeland.

This *Strategy* also calls on each of you. Every one of us should develop our own personal and family readiness plans to help protect us in the event of a natural or man-made disaster, enabling emergency responders and resources to be focused on those in greatest need.

Many of the threats we face – pandemic diseases, the proliferation of weapons of mass destruction, terrorism, and natural disasters – also demand multinational effort and cooperation. To this end, we have strengthened our homeland security through foreign partnerships, and we are committed to expanding and increasing our layers of defense, which extend well beyond our borders, by seeking further cooperation with our international partners.

As we secure the Homeland, however, we cannot simply rely on defensive approaches and well-planned response and recovery measures. We recognize that our efforts also must involve offense at home and abroad. We will disrupt the enemy's plans and diminish the impact of future disasters through measures that enhance the resilience of our economy and critical infrastructure before an incident occurs.

Today, our Nation is safer, but we are not yet safe. Since September 11, 2001, we have made great progress in confronting new challenges and refining our approach to homeland security. As acknowledged in 2002 in the first *National Strategy for Homeland Security*, we will not achieve all of our goals overnight, but we will achieve them. By the very nature of this struggle, many of our victories will be unheralded and achieved in silence.

Despite the difficult challenges ahead, we will fulfill our responsibility to safeguard America just as generations of Americans have before us. Together, guided by this *National Strategy for Homeland Security*, we will continue working to protect our families and communities, our liberty, and our way of life.

GEORGE W. BUSH

THE WHITE HOUSE

October 5, 2007

CONTENTS

Overview of America's
National Strategy for Homeland Security

America is at war with terrorist enemies who are intent on attacking our Homeland and destroying our way of life. The lives and livelihoods of the American people also remain at risk from natural catastrophes, including naturally occurring infectious diseases and hazards such as hurricanes and earthquakes, and man-made accidents. Our *National Strategy for Homeland Security* recognizes that while we must continue to focus on the persistent and evolving terrorist threat, we also must address the full range of potential catastrophic events, including man-made and natural disasters, due to their implications for homeland security.

The purpose of our *Strategy* is to guide, organize, and unify our Nation's homeland security efforts. It provides a common framework by which our entire Nation should focus its efforts on the following four goals:

- Prevent and disrupt terrorist attacks;

- Protect the American people, our critical infrastructure, and key resources;

- Respond to and recover from incidents that do occur; and

- Continue to strengthen the foundation to ensure our long-term success.

While the first three goals help to organize our national efforts, the last goal entails creating and transforming our homeland security principles, systems, structures, and institutions. This includes applying a comprehensive approach to risk management, building a culture of preparedness, developing a comprehensive Homeland Security Management System, improving incident management, better utilizing science and technology, and leveraging all instruments of national power and influence.

Homeland security requires a truly national effort, with shared goals and responsibilities for protecting and defending the Homeland. Our *Strategy* leverages the unique strengths and capabilities of all levels of government, the private and non-profit sectors, communities, and individual citizens. Mindful that many of the threats we face do not recognize geographic boundaries, we also will continue to work closely with our international partners throughout the world.

This updated *Strategy*, which builds directly from the first *National Strategy for Homeland Security* issued in July 2002, reflects our increased understanding of the terrorist threats confronting the United States today, incorporates lessons learned from exercises and real-world catastrophes – including Hurricane Katrina – and proposes new initiatives and approaches that will enable the Nation to achieve our homeland security objectives. This *Strategy* also complements both the *National Security Strategy* issued in March 2006 and the *National Strategy for Combating Terrorism* issued in September 2006.

Our first and most solemn obligation is to protect the American people. The *National Strategy for Homeland Security* will guide our Nation as we honor this commitment and achieve a more secure Homeland that sustains our way of life as a free, prosperous, and welcoming America.

Today's Realities in Homeland Security

Evolution of the Paradigm

The terrorist attacks on September 11, 2001, were acts of war against the United States and the principles of freedom, opportunity, and openness that define the American way of life. The severity and magnitude of the attacks were unprecedented, and that dark day became a watershed event in the Nation's approach to protecting and defending the lives and livelihoods of the American people.

Despite previous acts of terror on our Nation's soil – most notably the 1993 attack on the World Trade Center and the 1995 bombing of the Alfred P. Murrah Federal Building in Oklahoma City – homeland security before September 11 existed as a patchwork of efforts undertaken by disparate departments and agencies across all levels of government. While segments of our law enforcement and intelligence communities, along with our armed forces, assessed and prepared to act against terrorism and other significant threats to the United States, we lacked a unifying vision, a cohesive strategic approach, and the necessary institutions within government to secure the Homeland against terrorism.

> **Homeland Security Defined**
>
> Homeland Security is a concerted national effort to prevent terrorist attacks within the United States, reduce America's vulnerability to terrorism, and minimize the damage and recover from attacks that do occur.

The shock of September 11 transformed our thinking. In the immediate aftermath of history's deadliest international terrorist attack, we developed a homeland security strategy based on a concerted national effort to prevent terrorist attacks within the United States, reduce America's vulnerability to terrorism, and minimize the damage and recover from attacks that do occur. In order to help implement that strategy, we enhanced our homeland security and counterterrorism architecture at the Federal, State, local, Tribal, and community levels.

Our understanding of homeland security continued to evolve after September 11, adapting to new realities and threats. As we waged the War on Terror both at home and abroad, our Nation endured Hurricane Katrina, the most destructive natural disaster in U.S. history. The human suffering and staggering physical destruction caused by Katrina were a reminder that threats come not only from terrorism, but also from nature. Indeed, certain non-terrorist events that reach catastrophic levels can have significant implications for homeland security. The resulting national consequences and possible cascading effects from these events might present potential or perceived vulnerabilities that could be exploited, possibly eroding citizens' confidence in our Nation's government and ultimately increasing our vulnerability to attack. This *Strategy* therefore recognizes that effective preparation for catastrophic natural disasters and man-made disasters, while not homeland security *per se*, can nevertheless increase the security of the Homeland.

SHARED RESPONSIBILITY

Throughout the evolution of our homeland security paradigm, one feature most essential to our success has endured: the notion that homeland security is a shared responsibility built upon a foundation of partnerships. Federal, State, local, and Tribal governments, the private and non-profit sectors, communities, and individual citizens all share common goals and responsibilities – as well as accountability – for protecting and defending the Homeland.

The Federal Government as a united whole – and not simply one or two departments or agencies – has a critical role in homeland security and leads in those areas where it has a constitutional mandate or where it possesses the unique capabilities to address the most catastrophic or consequential scenarios. Those areas include, for example, border security; intelligence missions; and detecting, tracking, and rendering safe weapons of mass destruction (WMD). The Federal Government also is responsible for developing national strategies as well as promulgating best practices, national standards for homeland security, and national plans, as appropriate. It also uses targeted funding based on a risk management approach to help ensure that homeland security partners are capable of working together effectively and efficiently – in a truly national effort.

> ### State and Local Governments
>
> This *Strategy* defines "State" to mean any State of the United States, the District of Columbia, Puerto Rico, the Virgin Islands, Guam, American Samoa, the Commonwealth of the Northern Mariana Islands, or the trust territory of the Pacific Islands. This *Strategy* also defines "local government" as any county, city, village, town, district, or other political subdivision of any State, and includes any rural community or unincorporated town or village or any other public entity for which an application for assistance is made by a State or political subdivision thereof.

America's constitutional foundations of federalism and limited government place significant trust and responsibility in the capabilities of State and local governments to help protect the American people. State, local, and Tribal governments, which best understand their communities and the unique requirements of their citizens, provide our first response to incidents through law enforcement, fire, public health, and emergency medical services. They will always play a prominent, frontline role in helping to prevent terrorist attacks as well as in preparing for and responding to a range of natural and man-made emergencies.

The private and non-profit sectors also must be full partners in homeland security. As the country's principal providers of goods and services, and the owners or operators of approximately 85 percent of the Nation's critical infrastructure, businesses have both an interest in and a responsibility for ensuring their own security. The private sector plays key roles in areas as diverse as supply chain security, critical infrastructure protection, and research and development in science, technology, and other innovations that will help secure the Homeland. The non-profit sector, including volunteer and relief groups and faith-based organizations, provides important support services for the Nation, including meals and shelter, counseling, and compassion and comfort to Americans, particularly in the aftermath of an incident.

In order to complete this truly national effort, we also must encourage and draw upon an informed and active citizenry. For instance, citizens should each understand what to do if they observe suspicious behavior in their community and what to do in the event of an attack or natural disaster – this will reduce the threat to lives and property as well as the burden on emergency managers and first responders.

Partnerships in homeland security also extend beyond our Nation's borders. International cooperation continues to be an enduring feature of our approach to terrorism and violent extremism, infectious diseases, and other threats that transcend jurisdictional and geographic boundaries. The United States will continue to develop and strengthen foreign partnerships and the homeland security capabilities of our friends and allies. Security at home ultimately is related to security abroad: as partners protect and defend their homelands, the security of our own Homeland increases.

PROGRESS IN HOMELAND SECURITY AND BEYOND

We recognize that to the American people, progress should be measured not simply in terms of published plans or increased budgets; rather, it must be measured by the results that we achieve. Since September 11, we have made extraordinary progress, with most of our important successes in the War on Terror and in the full range of homeland security activities having been achieved through effective national and international partnerships. Our work, however, is far from over.

- We have greatly increased worldwide counterterrorism efforts since September 11, which has constrained the ability of al-Qaida to attack the Homeland and has led terrorist groups to find that the Homeland is a harder target to strike. These measures have helped disrupt multiple potentially deadly plots against the United States since September 11.

- We have instituted an active, multi-layered approach to securing the Homeland that integrates the capabilities of local, Tribal, State, and Federal governments, as well as those of the private and non-profit sectors, in order to secure the land, maritime, air, space, and cyber domains.

- We have made our borders more secure and developed an effective system of layered defense by strengthening the screening of people and goods overseas and by tracking and disrupting the international travel of terrorists.

- We have strengthened our ability to protect the American people by enhancing our homeland security and counterterrorism architecture through the creation of the Department of Homeland Security, the Office of the Director of National Intelligence, the Homeland Security Council, the National Counterterrorism Center, and U.S. Northern Command, a Department of Defense combatant command focused on homeland defense and civil support.

- The Federal Bureau of Investigation (FBI) and the Department of Justice (DOJ) have made the prevention of terrorist attacks their highest priority, as evidenced by the creation of the FBI's new National Security Branch and DOJ's new National Security Division. We also have more effectively leveraged State, local, and Tribal law enforcement efforts as part of our national homeland security enterprise.

- Through the targeted risk-based delivery of Federal grant funding and technical assistance, we have enhanced State, local, and Tribal homeland security training and equipment, emergency management capabilities, and the interoperability of communications.

- We have taken a series of historic steps to address biological threats, both deliberate and natural. These steps include unprecedented efforts to develop and procure medical countermeasures against bioterrorism and pandemic threats, improve capabilities for the detection of and response to biological attacks, and support State, local, and Tribal preparedness efforts through funding and explicit guidance.

- We have worked with the Congress to create, implement, and renew key legal reforms – such as the USA PATRIOT Act, the Intelligence Reform and Terrorism Prevention Act of 2004, and the Protect America Act of 2007 – which promote security and help to implement both the 9/11 Commission and the WMD Commission recommendations while protecting our fundamental liberties. Furthermore, with the Military Commissions Act of 2006, the United States can prosecute captured terrorists for war crimes through full and fair trials.

- Since September 11, the Administration has worked with the Congress to establish the Privacy and Civil Liberties Oversight Board as an integral part of the Executive Branch, and we have further established privacy officers in departments and agencies across the Federal Government – all to ensure that the rights of American citizens are considered and respected in our counterterrorism efforts.

- We have created a full-scale, comprehensive National Exercise Program to increase our preparedness to respond to the consequences of terrorist attacks and natural disasters.

CHALLENGES IN HOMELAND SECURITY AND BEYOND

While America is safer, we are not yet safe. Because of determined terrorist enemies and nature's unyielding power, significant challenges remain, including:

- The War on Terror remains a generational struggle, and our entire Nation must be engaged and prepared to participate in this effort.

- Terrorists have declared their intention to acquire and use weapons of mass destruction (WMD) to inflict catastrophic attacks against the United States and our allies, partners, and other interests.

- Our vast land and maritime borders make it difficult to completely deny terrorists and their weapons access to the Homeland.

- The United States is not immune to the emergence of homegrown radicalization and violent Islamic extremism.

- We must counter potential waning in the sense of urgency and levels of international cooperation as September 11 becomes a more distant memory and perceptions of the terrorist threat diverge.

- We must guard against complacency and balance the sense of optimism that is fundamental to the American character with the sober recognition that despite our best efforts, future catastrophes – natural and man-made – will occur, and thus we must always remain a prepared Nation.

- Although we have substantially improved our cooperation and partnership among all levels of government, private and non-profit sectors, communities, and individual citizens, we must continue to strengthen efforts to achieve full unity of effort through a stronger and further integrated national approach to homeland security.

- Although we have improved our ability to manage the risks that we face in the 21st century global security environment, we must enhance our ability to measure risk in a consistent and commonly accepted fashion and allocate finite resources accordingly.

- We must make additional reforms to the Foreign Intelligence Surveillance Act (FISA) and ensure that the statute is permanently amended so that our intelligence professionals continue to have the legal tools they need to gather information about the intentions of our enemies while protecting the civil liberties of Americans.

- While our information sharing capabilities have improved significantly, substantial obstacles remain. We must continue to break down information barriers among Federal, State, local, and Tribal partners and the private sector.

- The Congress must better align its oversight and committee structure in order to reflect the need for streamlined and effective legislative action that supports a unified approach to securing the Nation.

Today's Threat Environment

Our Nation faces complex and dynamic threats from terrorism. In addition, other threats from catastrophic events – including natural disasters, accidents, and other hazards – exist and must be addressed. We will continue to advance our understanding of these threats so we are better able to safeguard the American people.

Terrorism

Despite concerted worldwide efforts in the aftermath of September 11 that have disrupted terrorist plots and constrained al-Qaida's ability to strike the Homeland, the United States faces a persistent and evolving terrorist threat, primarily from violent Islamic terrorist groups and cells.

Currently, the most serious and dangerous manifestation of this threat remains al-Qaida, which is driven by an undiminished strategic intent to attack our Homeland. Although earlier efforts in the War on Terror deprived al-Qaida of its safe haven in Afghanistan and degraded its network by capturing or killing most of those responsible for September 11, the group has protected its top leadership, replenished operational lieutenants, and regenerated a safe haven in Pakistan's Federally Administered Tribal Areas – core capabilities that would help facilitate another attack on the Homeland.

Al-Qaida likely will continue to enhance its ability to attack America through greater cooperation with regional terrorist groups, particularly al-Qaida in Iraq – currently the group's most visible and capable affiliate and the only one known to have expressed a desire to attack us here. Moreover, although we have discovered only a handful of individuals in the United States with ties to al-Qaida senior leadership, the group likely will intensify its efforts to place operatives here in the Homeland. We also must never lose sight of al-Qaida's persistent desire for weapons of mass destruction, as the group continues to try to acquire and use chemical, biological, radiological, or nuclear material.

In addition to al-Qaida, a host of other groups and individuals also use terror and violence against the innocent in pursuit of their objectives and pose potential threats to the security of the United States. These include Lebanese Hizballah, which has conducted anti-U.S. attacks outside the United States and, prior to September 11, was responsible for more American deaths than any other terrorist organization. Hizballah may increasingly consider attacking the Homeland if it perceives the United States as posing a direct threat to the group or Iran, its principal sponsor.

The United States also is not immune to the emergence of homegrown radicalization and violent Islamic extremism within its borders. The arrest and prosecution inside the United States of a small number of violent Islamic extremists points to the possibility that others in the Homeland may become sufficiently radicalized to view the use of violence within the United States as legitimate. While our constitutional protection of freedom of religion, history of welcoming and assimilating new immigrants, strong economic opportunities, and equal-opportunity protections may help to mitigate the threat, drivers of radicalization still exist.

We will continue efforts to defeat this threat by working with Muslim American communities that stand at the forefront of this fight.

The terrorist threat to the Homeland is not restricted to violent Islamic extremist groups. We also confront an ongoing threat posed by domestic terrorists based and operating strictly within the United States. Often referred to as "single-issue" groups, they include white supremacist groups, animal rights extremists, and eco-terrorist groups, among others.

CATASTROPHIC NATURAL DISASTERS

Our *National Strategy for Homeland Security* recognizes that the lives and livelihoods of the American people also are at risk from natural catastrophes. Our vast Nation, with its varied population, geography, and landscape, will continue to endure a range of natural hazards and disasters.

Naturally occurring infectious diseases pose a significant and ongoing hazard. Increasing human contact with domesticated and wild animals (from which many human diseases emerge), the growing speed and volume of global travel and commerce, and a decline in the development of new infectious disease therapeutics complicate this challenge. In 2003, Severe Acute Respiratory Syndrome (SARS) demonstrated the potential for a global impact of a novel infectious disease. Originating in rural China, SARS resulted in more than 8,000 infections and 800 deaths worldwide and significant economic and social disruptions. The emergence of another novel disease without a known countermeasure, or a new influenza pandemic, could have dramatically greater consequences. Influenza pandemics have occurred intermittently over the centuries. The last three pandemics – in 1918, 1957, and 1968 – killed approximately 40 million, two million, and one million people worldwide, respectively. Although the timing cannot be predicted, history and science suggest that we will face one or more pandemics in this century.

Natural disasters also encompass a variety of meteorological and geological hazards. Hurricanes, for example, account for seven of the ten most costly disasters in U.S. history, including Hurricane Katrina – the Nation's most destructive natural disaster. While experts differ on the predicted intensity and frequency of future storms, history suggests the question is not if, but when, a devastating hurricane will reach our shores again. Earthquakes also will continue to be part of the hazard landscape. Although major advances have been achieved in understanding and mitigating earthquake hazards, Americans in 39 States face significant risk from earthquakes. Additionally, although each incident is often less significant than major hurricanes and earthquakes, floods are the most frequently occurring natural disaster and the leading cause of property damage and death from natural disasters in the Homeland over the past century. In an average year, more than 800 tornadoes are reported nationwide, resulting in 80 deaths and more than 1,500 injuries. In addition, wildfires remain a persistent hazard throughout many regions of the country.

CATASTROPHIC ACCIDENTS AND OTHER HAZARDS

We also remain vulnerable to catastrophic domestic accidents involving industrial hazards and infrastructure failures. These include the thousands of chemical spills that occur each year with the potential for significant public health and environmental impacts. In addition, incidents that pose potential threats to our Nation's critical infrastructure can lead to significant cascading effects across multiple systems. For example, an estimated 50 million people across eight States and the Canadian province of Ontario were left without electrical power in August 2003 when a utility in Ohio experienced problems that began a chain reaction of events leading to power outages lasting, in some places, several days. This incident, known as the "Northeast Blackout of 2003," cost roughly $6 billion and caused at least 265 power plants to shut down.

OUR VISION AND STRATEGY FOR HOMELAND SECURITY

We are a Nation blessed with unprecedented liberty, opportunity, and openness – foundations of the American way of life. Our principal terrorist enemies – al-Qaida, its affiliates, and those inspired by them – seek to destroy this way of life. Al-Qaida's plotting against our Homeland, for instance, focuses on prominent political, economic, and infrastructure targets designed to produce mass casualties, visually dramatic destruction, significant economic damage, fear, and loss of confidence in government among our population. Catastrophic events, including natural disasters and man-made accidents, also can produce similar devastating consequences that require an effective and coordinated national effort.

The United States, through a concerted national effort that galvanizes the strengths and capabilities of Federal, State, local, and Tribal governments; the private and non-profit sectors; and regions, communities, and individual citizens – along with our partners in the international community – will work to achieve a secure Homeland that sustains our way of life as a free, prosperous, and welcoming America.

In order to realize this vision, the United States will use all instruments of national power and influence – diplomatic, information, military, economic, financial, intelligence, and law enforcement – to achieve our goals to prevent and disrupt terrorist attacks; protect the American people, critical infrastructure, and key resources; and respond to and recover from incidents that do occur. We also will continue to create, strengthen, and transform the principles, systems, structures, and institutions we need to secure our Nation over the long term.

This is our strategy for homeland security.

PREVENT AND DISRUPT TERRORIST ATTACKS

In the aftermath of the September 11 attacks, the United States, together with partners across the globe, has waged an unrelenting War on Terror both to hold the perpetrators accountable and to prevent the recurrence of similar atrocities on any scale, whether at home or abroad.

The updated *National Strategy for Combating Terrorism*, released in September 2006, articulates our strategy for winning the War on Terror. Over the short term we are working to prevent attacks by terrorist networks, deny weapons of mass destruction (WMD) to rogue states and terrorists who seek to use them, deny terrorists the support and sanctuary of rogue states, and deny terrorists control of any nation they would use as a base and launching pad for terror. From the beginning, however, we recognized that the War on Terror is a different kind of war – not only a battle of arms but also a battle of ideas. Accordingly, we are advancing effective democracy as the antidote to the ideology of our terrorist enemies and the long-term solution for winning the War on Terror.

This *National Strategy for Homeland Security* is a companion to the *National Strategy for Combating Terrorism*, and the sections in both on preventing and disrupting terrorist attacks are complementary and mutually reinforcing. In order to prevent and disrupt terrorist attacks in the United States, we are working to deny terrorists and terrorist-related weapons and materials entry into our country and across all international borders, disrupt their ability to operate within our borders, and prevent the emergence of violent Islamic radicalization in order to deny terrorists future recruits and defeat homegrown extremism.

Preventing WMD Terrorism

The intent of our principal terrorist enemies to inflict catastrophic damage on the United States, coupled with their demonstrated contempt for human life, has fueled their desire to acquire WMD. Among our most important missions in denying entry to terrorists, their weapons, and other implements of terror is to detect, disrupt, and interdict the movement of WMD-related materials into the Homeland. This is one objective in our comprehensive strategy to prevent WMD terrorism, which is fully discussed in the *National Strategy for Combating Terrorism*. By integrating the operational and intelligence efforts of all levels of government, the private sector, and our foreign partners, and enabled by an international framework and domestic institutions supporting its implementation, our strategy involves simultaneous action to:

- Determine terrorists' intentions, capabilities, and plans to develop or acquire WMD;

- Deny terrorists access to the material, expertise, and other enabling capabilities required to develop WMD;

- Deter terrorists from employing WMD;

- Detect and disrupt terrorists' attempted movement of WMD-related materials, weapons, and personnel;

- Prevent and respond to a WMD-related terrorist attack; and

- Define the nature and source of a terrorist-employed WMD device.

WMD in the hands of terrorists is one of the gravest threats we face, and we cannot permit the world's most dangerous terrorists to threaten us with the world's most destructive weapons.

Deny Terrorists, Their Weapons, and Other Terror-Related Materials Entry to the Homeland

Denying our terrorist enemies the ability to travel internationally and, particularly, across and within our borders, severely inhibits their effectiveness. By preventing terrorists and their implements of destruction from entering the United States, we hinder their ability to identify and surveil possible targets, conduct planning, and launch an attack within our Homeland. Our *National Strategy to Combat Terrorist Travel*, *National Strategy for Maritime Security*, and *National Strategy for Aviation Security* are helping to guide our efforts. While we have strengthened travel and document security, improved information sharing with our domestic and international partners, and enhanced the screening of all visitors and cargo to the United States, our principal terrorist enemies are determined to infiltrate operatives and attack us on our soil. They also remain adaptive, exploiting perceived weaknesses in our dynamic travel system and using illicit means to circumvent our border and transportation security. We will defeat terrorists' efforts to infiltrate our Homeland while continuing to promote the reliable and efficient flow of people, goods, and services across our borders that is essential to American openness and economic prosperity.

- *Prevent terrorist exploitation of legitimate pathways into the Homeland.* Continuing to strengthen our layered system of protections that start overseas and continue along our borders, at our ports, on our roadways and railways, and in our skies is fundamental to preventing terrorists, their weapons, and related materials from entering our country through exploitation of legitimate pathways. In order to do this, we must continue to act deliberately on several fronts. A critical component of screening people is travel document security, because official documents are the key enablers for screening all people at ports of entry. The Western Hemisphere Travel Initiative and

Border Security and Interior Enforcement

As part of our broader effort for comprehensive immigration reform, we will work to further secure the Homeland and disrupt terrorist and other criminal activity in the United States. This includes improving our ability to detain and remove criminal and fugitive aliens and visa violators. We will continue to hire, train, and deploy additional Border Patrol agents, Customs and Border Protection officers, and Immigration and Customs Enforcement officers, as well as to build on the substantial improvements to the infrastructure and technology deployed at our borders. Additionally, we will expand detention bed space for aliens subject to detention and removal.

At the same time, we will enhance interior enforcement efforts, including worksite enforcement programs. Employers should be required to verify the work eligibility of all employees, preventing illegal immigrants from obtaining jobs through fraud or the use of stolen identification, including Social Security numbers. In order to accomplish this, we must expand the use of an electronic employment eligibility verification system that is timely, accurate, and easy for employers to use. We also will continue to crack down on employers who knowingly hire illegal immigrants by applying criminal penalties to those who circumvent the law. In addition, we will continue to step up efforts to verify the status of non-immigrants studying in the United States through the Student and Exchange Visitor Information System (SEVIS) and have appropriate follow-up where there may be violations. Taken together, these efforts will reinforce significantly enhanced border and interior security and help deny employment to those who are present in our country illegally, including criminals and potential terrorists.

the REAL ID Act are additional efforts to improve the integrity of documents used for entry into the United States. Enhancing international security standards through the use of biometrics, including in passports and visas, has made it increasingly difficult to counterfeit travel documents, and we must encourage those countries not in the Visa Waiver Program to adopt biometric passports. In the face of resourceful terrorists, however, we must continue to expand the US-VISIT program's biometric enrollment from two fingerprints to ten fingerprints, as well as leverage science and technology to enable more advanced multi-modal biometric recognition capabilities in the future that use fingerprint, face, or iris data. In order to further enhance travel document security, we will continue to press our international partners to strengthen and fully enforce laws criminalizing the counterfeiting, alteration, and misuse of identification and travel documents, and

> ## Screening People
>
> - The **REAL ID Act** establishes Federal standards for State-issued driver's licenses and non-driver's identification cards.
>
> - **Secure Flight** will require airlines to submit passenger information to DHS for flights that operate to, from, and within the United States, as well as those that fly over the continental United States.
>
> - The **Student and Exchange Visitor Information System** (SEVIS) is an internet-based system that is improving America's ability to track and monitor foreign students and exchange visitors.
>
> - The **United States Visitor and Immigrant Status Indicator Technology** (US-VISIT) program, when fully implemented, will create an entry and exit system that matches foreign travelers' arrival and departure records using biometrics to screen applicants for admission to the United States.
>
> - The **Western Hemisphere Travel Initiative** (WHTI) reduces the number of identification and citizenship documents that may be used by persons entering or re-entering the United States, from more than 8,000 documents, to a few dozen secure documents. This expedites document review at ports of entry while combating fraudulent documents.
>
> - The **Visa Waiver Program** (VWP) enables nationals of over two dozen countries to travel to the United States for tourism or business for stays of 90 days or less without obtaining a visa.

to report lost and stolen passports in a timely manner. These efforts build on the Department of State's screening for fraudulent passports and other documents through the visa interview process and U.S. Customs and Border Protection's examination of passports and visas for evidence of fraud during the admissions process.

By improving the screening of visa applicants, we also can help control access through ports of entry. Improved screening means enhancing our ability to more effectively identify prospective travelers who pose security threats through improved interview techniques, background checks, and the collection and comparison of biometrics. This includes expanding the use of security personnel abroad who are focused on assessing security threats and fraudulent documents used in the visa application process. It also means that we will continue to work with our foreign partners to share terrorist watchlists and to ensure other relevant electronic databases are accurate, up-to-date, and well-managed.

Terrorists also can exploit the global supply chains through which cargo enters the United States to smuggle their tools of terror, including possibly WMD. To counter this potential infiltration, and particularly to prevent the introduction of nuclear and radiological material into the Homeland, we will continue to expand the type of information we collect and improve cargo screening, scanning, and detection procedures and systems at foreign ports. Enhancing the Container Security Initiative, Megaports Initiative, and Secure Freight Initiative, among other international, multilateral, and bilateral efforts, is an important step toward developing a more robust global inspection and detection architecture for the 21st century. We will combine these efforts with strengthened interdiction measures for all types of cargo and all modes of transport to further constrain the mobility of terrorists, their weapons, and other material. We also will

> ### Screening Cargo
>
> - The **Container Security Initiative** (CSI) creates a security regime to prescreen and evaluate maritime containers – before they are shipped from foreign ports – through automated targeting tools, ensuring that high-risk cargo is examined or scanned.
>
> - The **Customs-Trade Partnership Against Terrorism** (C-TPAT) is a voluntary U.S. Customs and Border Protection program whereby participating businesses undergo a review of security procedures and adopt enhanced security measures in order to expedite shipping.
>
> - The **Megaports Initiative** is a Department of Energy program in which the United States collaborates with foreign trade partners to enhance their ability to scan cargo for nuclear and other radiological materials at major international seaports.
>
> - The **Secure Freight Initiative** is a comprehensive model for securing the global supply chain that seeks to enhance security while keeping legitimate trade flowing. It leverages shipper information, host country government partnerships, and trade partnerships to scan cargo containers bound for the United States.

continue to strengthen and enhance screening, scanning, and detection capabilities at all U.S. maritime ports and land ports of entry for cargo entering, leaving, and moving within the country.

Additionally, in order to improve the security of international commercial systems and supply chains, the United States will enhance the Customs-Trade Partnership Against Terrorism to further develop public-private partnerships with the full range of partners involved in commerce and transportation. The private sector is central to improving security along the entire supply chain – from the factory floor to foreign vendors, at seaports, and across borders. This integrated public-private partnership also will be important in stimulating the development and implementation of best practices, risk management approaches, and industry codes of conduct. Risk assessment is a critical element of corporate valuations, so companies that minimize risk will be rewarded by the market.

- *Prevent terrorist use of illicit pathways into the Homeland.* While some terrorists will continue to exploit legitimate channels to move personnel and weapons into and within our country, others might attempt to infiltrate our land, maritime, and air borders by car, truck, rail, foot, boat, or aircraft. In order to disrupt the use of illicit pathways into the Homeland, we will continue to implement an integrated system of people, technology, and tactical infrastructure through the Secure Border Initiative to detect, identify, respond to, and resolve illegal entry attempts at our land borders. We also will enhance and improve the coordination of surveillance of watercraft and general aviation. We will work with our neighbors and international partners to shrink the illicit travel networks used by human smugglers, narco-traffickers, and other transnational criminals whose activities foster continued exploitation of our borders.

DISRUPT TERRORISTS AND THEIR CAPACITY TO OPERATE IN THE UNITED STATES

The United States and our partners and allies are attacking terrorists and their networks in a campaign of direct and continuous action to deny them what they need to operate and survive overseas. We are on the offense at home, too – taking the fight to an enemy that exploits our open and diverse society, hides among us, and tries to attack us from within. Leveraging our Nation's foundation of homeland security partnerships, as well as our relationships with committed friends across the globe, we will work to uncover terrorists and terrorist activity within our borders and take swift and effective action to preempt and disrupt their activities and enterprises. The Federal Government must ensure that we have the necessary and appropriate legal tools to accomplish these objectives while at the same time preserving the rights and civil liberties of all Americans.

- *Identify and locate terrorists and uncover terrorist activity.* In order to uncover terrorists and terrorist activity against the backdrop of our highly mobile, dynamic, and diverse society, we must attain domain awareness of the actions, events, and trends that occur throughout our land, maritime, air, space, and cyber domains. This is a multifaceted process. First, partners throughout the entire law enforcement community must continue to enhance their baseline understanding of their operating environments – the people, the geography, and the daily and weekly rhythm of activities and events. By understanding trend lines, we can better identify anomalies and deviations that could indicate terrorist activity. The reporting of unusual or suspicious activity by private sector partners and a vigilant public also is essential to this effort. Identifying terrorists and detecting terrorist activity and plotting also require a greater understanding of how suspect activities at the local level relate to the strategic environment. Our law enforcement and intelligence communities must have detailed knowledge of our Homeland adversaries, including their identities, sources of support, intentions, capabilities, and modi operandi. This information must be assessed against a current strategic threat picture that continues to integrate national intelligence.

  In order to enhance our domain awareness as well as improve our understanding of how terrorist enemies are likely to operate in the Homeland, the law enforcement community, along with the intelligence community, must work to develop and imple-

> ### Intelligence-Led Policing
>
> Intelligence-Led Policing (ILP) is a management and resource allocation approach to law enforcement using data collection and intelligence analysis to set specific priorities for all manner of crimes, including those associated with terrorism. ILP is a collaborative approach based on improved intelligence operations and community-oriented policing and problem solving, which the field of law enforcement has considered beneficial for many years. Today it is being adopted by a variety of law enforcement entities.

ment national information requirements – developing a process for identifying information gaps, determining critical information requirements, and meeting those requirements collaboratively. We also must encourage the implementation of Intelligence-Led Policing by State, local, and Tribal law enforcement – after all, they best understand their communities, citizens, and current trend lines. Working in a collaborative environment, the Federal Government will recommend priorities for State, local, and Tribal homeland security activities that focus resources on the most pressing problems, adopt a formal intelligence process with requirements generation and tasking of information collection, and analyze and disseminate the information. Underlying our efforts to achieve domain awareness and identify and locate terrorists and terrorist activity in the Homeland is a fully developed and integrated Information Sharing Environment (see the chapter titled "Ensuring Long-Term Success") that supports the vertical and horizontal distribution of terrorism-related information among Federal, State, local, Tribal, and foreign governments and the private sector, as appropriate.

- *Disrupt terrorists and their activities and networks.* As we achieve domain awareness throughout our communities, our Federal, State, local, and Tribal law enforcement authorities will collaborate to investigate, disrupt, and preempt terrorist activity and deny terrorists the capacity to operate effectively within our borders. This means targeting all elements of a network that terrorists need to operate and survive. For instance, we will investigate, arrest, and prosecute or, where appropriate, remove terrorist leaders, operatives, facilitators, and trainers. We also will freeze or seize terrorist funds, disrupt funding sources, and interdict their financing transfer mechanisms. Furthermore, we will focus on criminal behavior and other terrorist financing methodologies that terrorist groups or cells may use to finance or otherwise facilitate their activities.

> ### Improvised Explosive Devices
>
> Over the past several years, al-Qaida – our principal terrorist enemy – has demonstrated its ability and intent to employ innovative weapons against U.S. interests, including in the Homeland, and our friends and allies overseas. The disrupted 2006 U.K.-based plot to blow up multiple trans-Atlantic commercial airliners with liquid explosives is especially noteworthy. We remain particularly concerned about the employment of improvised explosive devices (IEDs) in an attack against the Homeland, given the ready availability of IED components and the relative technological ease with which they can be fashioned. In conjunction with an array of activities to deny terrorists the weapons and tools they use to kill the innocent, our *National Strategy for Combating Terrorist Use of Explosives*, which is being developed pursuant to Homeland Security Presidential Directive-19 (issued February 12, 2007), will help guide our efforts.

We also will work with domestic and international partners to deny terrorists what they need to operate in the Homeland, including the weapons and tools they use to kill the innocent. These include missiles, rockets, explosives, and small arms acquired through a variety of means, including theft, fraud, state sponsor support, and black market purchases. Terrorists and their state sponsors also may exploit dual-use technologies, including technologies that are being used for great benefit in medicine, agriculture, and industry. We will stringently enforce our export control laws as a means of denying rogue actors – including terrorist groups – access to restricted dual-use items. We will work with our private sector and international partners to ensure the presence of industry standards, national systems of oversight, and penalties for misuse of such items while preserving the advancement of science and technology to save lives and improve our quality of life.

Defeating terrorist activity in the Homeland also requires preventing terrorist exploitation of our financial, cyber, and legal systems. Terrorists use financial systems to raise, store, and transfer funds that serve as the lifeblood of their operations. We have hardened U.S. financial systems against terrorist abuse by building upon our anti-money laundering system and broadening and deepening safeguards in the international financial system while taking steps to deter and disrupt specific terrorist funding. We have done this in large part by building strong international law enforcement alliances and effective public-private partnerships committed to preventing the flow of illicit capital through formal and informal financial mechanisms. We will continue to strengthen this approach and use intelligence, law enforcement, and regulatory steps, such as our targeted financial sanctions, to identify and isolate actors involved in terrorist financing.

Terrorists also seek sanctuary in the cyber domain, particularly the Internet, an inexpensive, geographically unbounded, and largely unconstrained virtual haven for our enemies. Terrorists use the Internet to create and disseminate propaganda, recruit new members, raise funds, and plan operations. The Internet has become a training ground, with terrorists acquiring instruction once possible only through physical training camps. In addition to discrediting their terrorist propaganda on the Internet with the promotion of truthful messages, we will seek to deny the Internet to our terrorist enemies as an effective safe haven for their recruitment, fund-raising, training, and operational planning.

Foreign Intelligence Surveillance Act Modernization

Since its enactment in 1978, the Foreign Intelligence Surveillance Act (FISA), as amended, has provided a legal framework through which the Intelligence Community lawfully collects foreign intelligence information of value to our Nation's security, while simultaneously protecting the civil liberties of Americans. Revolutionary changes in technology since 1978 had the effect of expanding the scope of FISA's coverage to include foreign intelligence collection efforts that Congress did not intend to subject to the statute's requirements. This unintended expansion of FISA's scope meant that our intelligence professionals, in a significant number of cases, needed to obtain a court order to collect foreign intelligence information against a target located overseas. This circumstance created an unnecessary obstacle to our Intelligence Community's ability to gather real-time information about the intent of our enemies overseas and diverted scarce resources that would be better spent safeguarding the civil liberties of people in the United States, not foreign terrorists who wish to do us harm. The Protect America Act of 2007, which passed with bipartisan support in the House and the Senate, was an important interim step in modernizing FISA to account for modern changes in technology and the threats that we face in the 21st century. Working with Congress, we must make additional reforms to FISA and ensure that the statute is permanently amended so that our intelligence professionals continue to have the legal tools they need to gather information about the intentions of our enemies while protecting the civil liberties of Americans – now and in the future.

The United States has a domestic legal system that supports the investigation and prosecution of terrorist activities while simultaneously protecting individual privacy, the First Amendment rights of association, religious freedom, and free speech, and other civil liberties. We are a Nation built on the rule of law, and we will apply our laws to defeat terrorism while always preserving our liberties. Toward that end, not only must we guard against any gaps in our system that would offer terrorists a virtual haven to exploit, but we also must ensure that our law enforcement community has the necessary and proper mix of tools and authorities to defeat the threats of the 21st century.

PREVENT VIOLENT ISLAMIC EXTREMIST RADICALIZATION IN THE UNITED STATES

The arrest and prosecution inside the United States of a small number of violent Islamic extremists demonstrates that we are not immune to the emergence of homegrown violent Islamic extremism. Potential catalysts for radicalization within Muslim American communities include feelings or perceptions of social discrimination that generate a sense of alienation from society and distrust of the government; perceptions of political and economic inequalities; and dissatisfaction with foreign and domestic U.S. policies viewed as hostile to Muslims. Preventing and disrupting radicalization requires concerted, focused action in the near term. While our *Strategy* focuses on preventing homegrown violent Islamic extremism – the ideology underpinning the principal terrorist threat confronting the United States today – we recognize that terrorists and violent extremists can arise in many other faiths, communities, or persuasions. Accordingly, our *Strategy* can be appropriately tailored to address a variety of domestic communities and groups whose members may be susceptible to radicalization.

- *Engage key communities as partners in the War on Terror.* Our *Strategy* recognizes the centrality of the very people our terrorist enemies most want to exploit: the faithful followers of Islam. The fact that our country has not experienced the level of homegrown violent Islamic extremism that has begun to plague other Western democracies is, in large measure, a tribute to American society, which values free expression and encourages all to engage politically and economically. As the primary targets of radicalization who stand at the forefront of the struggle against violent extremism, Muslim Americans are uniquely situated to offer insights and solutions. More broadly, community engagement and public-private partnerships across American society are essential to our success. We will continue to strengthen grassroots dialogue and interaction among Muslim communities and all levels of government, as well as with non-Muslim sectors of our society, because Americans of all religions, races, and ethnicities have a stake and role to play in the War on Terror. Engagement, taking place through public-private task forces and forums, includes work to ensure the preservation of liberty and religious pluralism and the enforcement of civil rights and hate crimes laws, discussions about U.S. foreign and domestic policy concerns, and addressing the ability of Muslim Americans to fulfill obligations of charitable giving, international travel, and religious practice.

- *Identify and counter the sources of radicalization.* The purveyors of violent extremism rely upon access to targeted communities to inculcate and spread their ideology. Law enforcement officials, therefore, must continue to identify and address sources of violent extremist radicalization in the Homeland. One place where we have already witnessed radicalization is in our prison system, but we must continue to identify other places violent propagators exploit within the United States, overseas, and on the Internet. In order to counter sources of radicalization, we will continue to support community and grassroots initiatives that publicly condemn the use of violence in general and specific acts of terror whenever and wherever they occur, debunk the claim of our terrorist enemies that the United States is at war with Islam, and counter all forms of propaganda that distort and misrepresent U.S. policy by clearly communicating U.S. policies – what they mean, how and why they are carried out, and how they affect all Americans. We also will support community and grassroots efforts to promote the values of citizenship, democracy, integration, religious tolerance, and the protection of civil rights, as well as increase cooperation among Tribal, State, and Federal prison officials and Muslim communities to counter radicalization in prisons.

- *Enhance Federal, State, local, and Tribal government capacities to address radicalization.* All levels of our government must strengthen institutions and human resources in a way that increases our ability to prevent violent Islamic extremism within our borders, identify when it is occurring, and spot new trends and developments in the radicalization process. To that end, we will continue to educate and train law enforcement and other U.S. Government personnel on Islamic cultural and community norms as well as prioritize the recruitment and retention of those having relevant language skills and cultural backgrounds; educate Federal, State, local, and Tribal government personnel on radicalization, expand current training programs on cultural proficiency, and encourage interagency training and career opportunities to facilitate the development and sharing of expertise; and improve interagency cooperation and information sharing at all levels of government.

- *Continue to advance our understanding of radicalization.* As we achieve success in preventing homegrown violent Islamic extremism, we should expect our adaptive enemies to create new methods for spreading their ideology of hate and murder. In order to identify and preempt new trends and developments, we will continue to advance our knowledge and understanding of radicalization by supporting relevant public and private research, including with regard to the vulnerabilities or susceptibility of individuals to violent Islamic extremism. Furthermore, we will keep working with Muslim communities to improve our understanding of the sources and evolving trends of radicalization and identify how changing technologies could affect radicalization.

Protect the American People, Critical Infrastructure, and Key Resources

W hile protecting the lives and livelihoods of the American people demands that we work to prevent and disrupt terrorist attacks in the Homeland, it also requires that we undertake measures to deter the threat of terrorism, mitigate the Nation's vulnerabilities, and minimize the consequences of an attack or disaster should it occur. Our efforts include, among other things, protecting our population from infectious diseases and catastrophic public health threats, as well as reducing the effects and consequences of all hazards through improved systems to notify, alert, and warn the public.

Safeguarding the American people also includes the preservation of the Nation's critical infrastructure and key resources (CI/KR). As set forth in the 2006 *National Infrastructure Protection Plan* (NIPP), critical infrastructure includes the assets, systems, and networks, whether physical or virtual, so vital to the United States that their incapacitation or destruction would have a debilitating effect on security, national economic security, public health or safety, or any combination thereof. Key resources are publicly or privately controlled resources essential to the minimal

---

Protection and Risk Management

Despite our best efforts, achieving a complete state of CI/KR protection is not possible in the face of the numerous and varied catastrophic possibilities that could challenge the security of America today. Recognizing that the future is uncertain and that we cannot envision or prepare for every potential threat, we must understand and accept a certain level of risk as a permanent condition. Managing homeland security risk requires a disciplined approach to resource prioritization and the diversification of protective responsibilities across the full spectrum of our Nation's homeland security partners. Applying a risk-based framework to all homeland security efforts will help to ensure our success over the long term and is discussed in detail in the chapter titled "Ensuring Long-Term Success."

---

operations of the economy and government. By protecting CI/KR, we further protect the American people and build a safer, more secure, and more resilient Nation.

Deter the Terrorist Threat

We seek to deter state sponsors of terrorism, terrorist groups, and other non-state actors who support or facilitate terrorism by undertaking various actions to decrease their likelihood of success as well as alter their motivational calculus.

- *Decreasing likelihood of success.* Terrorist actors can be deterred and dissuaded from conducting attacks if they perceive that they are not likely to achieve their objectives or that the costs of their efforts are too high. The counterterrorism and homeland security activities outlined in the chapter titled "Prevent and Disrupt Terrorist Attacks" are part of our deterrent strategy – making it increasingly difficult for our enemies to achieve their objective of an attack in the Homeland by denying them and their weapons entry to the United States, denying them the ability to operate effectively within our borders, and denying them future recruits by preventing homegrown radicalization.

As a protective function, this concept of "deterrence through denial" requires additional actions, including increased defensive postures at potential sites of attack. Prominent political, economic, and infrastructure targets are attractive to our enemies, as are large places of public gatherings and symbolic targets, such as national monuments. In order to deny terrorists access to potential targets and decrease their likelihood of success, the Federal Government, in full collaboration with State, local, Tribal, and private sector partners, will continue to harden sites, as appropriate, and strengthen security through the presence of security forces, reinforcement of defensive barriers, and enhancement of access control measures. The continued targeted provision of Federal assistance to State, local, and Tribal governments and the private sector – through risk- and performance-based criteria – will ensure that these entities receive the dollars and training necessary to effectively implement these measures. Additionally, the use of both active and passive countermeasures as well as their unpredictable application will help ensure greater effectiveness. We also must promote public awareness of our increased security practices so terrorists understand that we are increasing the likelihood that they will not succeed.

> ### The National Infrastructure Protection Plan
>
> Guiding our efforts to protect the Nation's CI/KR is the 2006 *National Infrastructure Protection Plan* (NIPP) and its supporting Sector-Specific Plans, which were developed pursuant to Homeland Security Presidential Directive-7, issued on December 17, 2003. The NIPP sets forth a comprehensive risk management framework and provides a coordinated approach to CI/KR protection roles and responsibilities for Federal, State, local, and private sector security partners. It sets national priorities, goals, and requirements for the effective distribution of funding and resources that will help ensure that our government, economy, and public services continue to function in the event of a man-made or natural disaster. In accordance with HSPD-7, the NIPP includes an augmented focus on the protection of CI/KR from the unique and potentially catastrophic effects of terrorist attacks. However, the NIPP framework supports a larger all-hazard approach to CI/KR protection.

Hardening sites against external threats is only one side of the deterrence equation. Terrorists also may seek to infiltrate or recruit an individual with privileged access to a hardened site. These insiders can offer our terrorist enemies information on exploitable vulnerabilities or even provide terrorist operatives access to sensitive or controlled areas. We must therefore continue to work with our State, local, Tribal, and private sector partners to review workforce surety programs and standards for screening and background checks, where appropriate. Finally, we must continue to conduct threat and vulnerability assessments and calibrate our defensive measures accordingly to account for changes in terrorists' strategic targeting, tactics, techniques, and procedures, as well as changes in the larger operating environment.

- *Changing motivational calculus.* Terrorist actors also can be deterred or dissuaded from conducting attacks if they fear potential consequences for their actions. Since September 11, the United States has made it clear that we and our partners in the War on Terror make no distinction between those who commit acts of terror and those who support and harbor them. Any government that chooses to be an ally of terror has chosen to be an enemy of freedom, justice, and peace, and we, along with our international partners, will hold our terrorist enemies to account.

Altering the calculus of our terrorist enemies – including all elements of the terrorist network – so that they fear the consequences of their actions requires credibility. We will continue to communicate and demonstrate our will to take action, both to our enemies in order to raise their awareness and to the American people so that they remain confident in our resolve. Maintaining our credibility also requires that we not only demonstrate our will to hold terrorists, their sponsors, and facilitators accountable, but that we also retain the capabilities and flexibility to do so. This includes enhancing our ability to respond to acts of terror using all instruments of national power, as well as refining our ability to define the nature, source, and perpetrator of an attack. To further strengthen the potential consequences our terrorist enemies face, we will continue to isolate and discredit those who support or facilitate terrorism, bring to justice terrorist actors, build a moral counterweight to undermine the perceived legitimacy of terrorism and the targeting of innocents, and ultimately create a global environment inhospitable to terrorists, violent extremists, and all who support them.

MITIGATE VULNERABILITIES

We will not be able to deter all terrorist threats, and it is impossible to deter or prevent natural catastrophes. We can, however, mitigate the Nation's vulnerability to acts of terrorism, other man-made threats, and natural disasters by ensuring the structural and operational resilience of our critical infrastructure and key resources and by further protecting the American people through medical preparedness.

- **Ensuring CI/KR structural resilience.** While the devastation of even one sector of our critical infrastructure or key resources would have a debilitating effect on our national security and possibly damage the morale and confidence of the American people, interdependencies make the protection of CI/KR particularly essential. A failure in one area, such as our water supply system, can adversely affect not only public health but

Critical Infrastructure and Key Resources
Our Nation has identified 17 sectors of critical infrastructure and key resources, each with cross-cutting physical, cyber, and human elements:
Agriculture and Food
Banking and Finance
Chemical
Commercial Facilities
Commercial Nuclear Reactors, Materials, and Waste
Dams
Defense Industrial Base
Drinking Water and Water Treatment Systems
Emergency Services
Energy
Government Facilities
Information Technology
National Monuments and Icons
Postal and Shipping
Public Health and Health Care
Telecommunications
Transportation Systems

also the ability of first responders to provide emergency services. Accordingly, ensuring the survivability of our CI/KR assets, systems, and networks requires that we continue to accurately model their interdependencies and better assess and understand the potential cascading effects that could impact and impede operations in interconnected infrastructures.

For each CI/KR sector, we must collectively work to ensure the ability of power, communications, and other life sustaining systems to survive an attack by terrorists, a natural disaster, and other assessed risks or hazards. In the past, investments in redundant and duplicative infrastructure were used to achieve this objective. We must now focus on the resilience of the system as a whole – an approach that centers on investments that make the system better able to absorb the impact of an event without losing the capacity to function. While this might include the building of redundant assets, resilience often is attained through the dispersal of key functions across multiple service providers and flexible supply chains and related systems. Resilience also includes the protection and physical survivability of key national assets and structures.

Additionally, an important aspect of promoting resilience includes seismic retrofitting and adherence to stricter building codes, as appropriate. Flood mitigation activities are also important and include the maintenance of flood plains. We also must increase participation in the National Flood Insurance Program and base that program on actuarial rates.

While the Federal Government provides overarching leadership and coordination for protecting and mitigating the vulnerabilities of our Nation's CI/KR, all partners in homeland security have impor-

---

Cyber Security: A Special Consideration

Many of the Nation's essential and emergency services, as well as our critical infrastructure, rely on the uninterrupted use of the Internet and the communications systems, data, monitoring, and control systems that comprise our cyber infrastructure. A cyber attack could be debilitating to our highly interdependent CI/KR and ultimately to our economy and national security.

A variety of actors threaten the security of our cyber infrastructure. Terrorists increasingly exploit the Internet to communicate, proselytize, recruit, raise funds, and conduct training and operational planning. Hostile foreign governments have the technical and financial resources to support advanced network exploitation and launch attacks on the informational and physical elements of our cyber infrastructure. Criminal hackers threaten our Nation's economy and the personal information of our citizens, and they also could pose a threat if wittingly or unwittingly recruited by foreign intelligence or terrorist groups. Our cyber networks also remain vulnerable to natural disasters.

In order to secure our cyber infrastructure against these man-made and natural threats, our Federal, State, and local governments, along with the private sector, are working together to prevent damage to, and the unauthorized use and exploitation of, our cyber systems. We also are enhancing our ability and procedures to respond in the event of an attack or major cyber incident. The *National Strategy to Secure Cyberspace* and the NIPP's Cross-Sector Cyber Security plan are guiding our efforts.

---

tant roles to play. This is especially true of the private sector, which owns and operates approximately 85 percent of the Nation's critical infrastructure and is the first line of defense for those assets. We will continue to strengthen our partnerships with State, local, and Tribal governments and the private sector so that we collectively can fulfill our responsibilities, as outlined in the NIPP, to protect and ensure the resilience of our Nation's most critical assets. Our partnerships also extend to our international neighbors. Many of our CI/KR assets are intertwined with a global infrastructure that has evolved to support modern economies. While this global system brings efficiencies and benefits, it also creates vulnerabilities and challenges, and we must continue to work with our partners across the globe to protect the structural resilience of what has become a system of systems at home and abroad.

- *Ensuring operational resilience.* Mitigating the vulnerability of government and private sector operations to man-made or natural disasters depends not only on the structural resilience of our assets, systems, and networks but also on operational resilience. First, we will continue to maintain comprehensive and effective continuity programs, including those that integrate continuity of operations and continuity of government programs, to ensure the preservation of our government under the Constitution and the continuing performance of national essential functions – those government roles that are necessary to lead and sustain the Nation during and following a catastrophic emergency. A national approach to continuity also requires that State, local, and Tribal governments work to ensure that they are able to maintain or rapidly resume effective functioning during and after catastrophic incidents and are able to interact effectively with each other and the Federal Government. Likewise, we strongly encourage the private sector to conduct business continuity planning that recognizes interdependencies and complements governmental efforts – doing so not only helps secure the United States, but also makes good long-term business sense for individual companies. Such integrated and comprehensive planning is essential to protecting and preserving lives and livelihoods and maintaining our robust economy during crises.

- *Protecting the American people through medical preparedness.* As we protect our Nation's critical infrastructure and key resources by working to deter terrorist threats and mitigate vulnerabilities through structural and operational resilience, we are helping to protect the American people. Our population, however, requires additional protective measures. We must reduce the vulnerability of the American populace to intentional dissemination of harmful biological agents, detonation of a nuclear or radiological device, the intentional or accidental release of toxic chemicals, naturally occurring infectious disease such as an influenza pandemic, and meteorological or geological events such as hurricanes or earthquakes.

Reducing the Nation's vulnerability to public health threats requires that we continue to build sustainable systems for prevention, detection, reporting, investigation, control, and recovery. We must continue to expand the capabilities of the public health and medical communities to identify and assess threats and to determine if an attack or outbreak has occurred – all in a rapid and reliable manner. In order to facilitate our efforts, we will continue to upgrade our systems for clinical surveillance and environmental monitoring, as well as ensure the effective and timely integration and sharing of data, conclusions, and other information with State, local, and Tribal authorities and other appropriate homeland security partners. Likewise, we will encourage the timely sharing of information learned at the State, local, and Tribal level with the Federal Government.

In order to further mitigate the vulnerability of the American people to natural or man-made health threats, we must ensure that we have access to the necessary medical countermeasures, appropriately enhancing and expanding our flexible medical toolkit against potential biological threats. We must facilitate States and local and Tribal communities in establishing appropriate levels of medical stockpiles and the systems that can rapidly distribute medical countermeasures to large, at-risk populations. Finally, we must assist communities as they develop medical systems that are able to sustain delivery of situation-appropriate care in the setting of catastrophic events. Like other homeland security activities, protecting the health of citizens is a shared responsibility – one that starts at the individual and family level, involves government and the private sector, and relies heavily on local action. While the Federal Government possesses unique tools and resources to guide and assist efforts to protect the health of citizens from all disasters, collaborative community and regional planning is essential for the protection of the American people.

MINIMIZE CONSEQUENCES

Despite our best deterrent and mitigation efforts, terrorist attacks and natural disasters will happen, and we must work to minimize the consequences of their occurrence. Several of our efforts to reduce our Nation's vulnerabilities necessarily reduce the consequences of a disaster. This is the mutually reinforcing nature of our integrated efforts to protect the American people, critical infrastructure, and key resources. Moreover, the core of our efforts to minimize consequences lies with our comprehensive approach for responding to and recovering from incidents, which is described in the next chapter.

There are, however, pre-incident steps that we can take that can help to further reduce the effects and consequences of those events that do occur and better protect the American people, particularly through improved notification, alert, and warning systems. We must continue to develop reliable, effective, and flexible national systems to warn Americans of impending threats, including acts of terrorism, natural disasters, acts of war, and other hazards to public security and well-being. Beyond press conferences and warnings through television and radio, these systems must leverage modern and changing technology to push vital information to citizens wherever they are. Pre-incident alerts and warnings should be geographically or functionally targeted and provide guidance and instruction so that governments, the private sector, and individual citizens can take necessary preparatory or protective actions. These messages should continue throughout and immediately after the event, providing situational updates and current directions, as appropriate.

Respond to and Recover from Incidents

Despite our comprehensive and steadfast efforts to prevent and disrupt terrorist attacks and protect the American people, critical infrastructure, and key resources, our terrorist enemies remain determined to destroy our way of life, and nature continues to release its destructive forces. Given the certainty of catastrophes on our soil – no matter how unprecedented or extraordinary – it is our collective duty to provide the best response possible. When needed, we will bring to bear the Nation's full capabilities and resources to save lives, mitigate suffering, and protect property. As the Nation responds based on the scope and nature of the incident, we must begin to lay the foundation not only for a strong recovery over the short term but also for the rebuilding and revitalization of affected communities and regions over the long term. This is crucial to reducing the psychological, social, and economic effects of an incident. Ultimately, response, recovery, and rebuilding efforts are tightly intertwined, each tapping into the resilience of the American spirit and our determination to endure and become stronger in the face of adversity.

In order to respond effectively to an incident and initiate short-term recovery, we must have a system that can quickly adapt to the full range of catastrophic scenarios confronting the Nation today and seamlessly integrate capabilities and resources from all stakeholders – Federal, State, local, and Tribal governments and the private and non-profit sectors – to achieve common objectives. At the core of our efforts have been the National Response Plan (now referred to as the National Response Framework) and the National Incident Management System (NIMS), which were developed pursuant to Homeland Security Presidential Directive-5, issued on February 28, 2003. Building on best practices, lessons learned from exercises and real-world events, including our response to Hurricane Katrina, and the ongoing formal review and revision of the National Response Framework, we will continue to improve our all-hazards approach for responding

> ### Incident Management Versus Response
>
> The homeland security community has used the terms "incident management" and "response" in complementary and occasionally interchangeable manners. Within this *Strategy*, "response" refers to actions taken in the immediate aftermath of an incident to save lives, meet basic human needs, and reduce the loss of property. "Incident management," however, is a broader concept that refers to how we manage incidents and mitigate consequences across all homeland security activities, including prevention, protection, and response and recovery. This concept, including the role of the National Incident Management System (NIMS), is discussed further in the chapter titled "Ensuring Long-Term Success."

to and recovering from incidents. Ultimately, our National Response Framework must help us strengthen the foundation for an effective national response, rapidly assess emerging incidents, take initial actions, expand operations as needed, and commence recovery actions to stabilize the area. This framework must be clearly written, easy to understand, and designed to be truly national in scope, meeting the needs of State, local, and Tribal governments and the private and non-profit sectors, as well as the Federal Government. We also will ensure that those communities devastated or severely affected by a catastrophic incident are set on a sustainable path for long-term rebuilding and revitalization.

Strengthen the Foundation for an Effective National Response

An effective all-hazards response effort must begin with a strong foundation based on clear roles and responsibilities across all levels of government and the private and non-profit sectors, strengthened doctrine to guide our national response, a joint planning process to improve response capabilities, and advance readiness activities to better prepare for an impending or emergent event. The effectiveness of our efforts will be determined by the people who fulfill key roles and how they carry out their responsibilities, including their commitment to develop plans and partnerships, conduct joint training and exercises, and achieve shared goals.

- *Clarify how national roles and responsibilities are fulfilled across all levels of government and the private and non-profit sectors.* Disaster response has traditionally been handled by State, local, and Tribal governments, with the Federal Government and private and non-profit sectors playing supporting and *ad hoc* roles, respectively. A lack of clarity regarding roles and responsibilities across these levels can lead to gaps and seams in our national response and delay our ability to provide life-saving support when needed. Accordingly, we must better articulate how roles, responsibilities, and lines of authority for all response stakeholders are fulfilled across all levels of government and among the private and nonprofit sectors so that each understands how it supports the broader national response. We will continue to base our Federal planning and response efforts on the premise that the vast majority of incidents will be handled at the lowest jurisdictional level possible, with the Federal Government anticipating needs and assisting State, local, and Tribal authorities upon request, when their capabilities are insufficient, or in special circumstances where Federal interests are directly implicated. Public-private partnerships also are essential, and we will work together to better define the roles that the private and non-profit sectors can play, particularly in their local communities, to achieve a more successful response.

- *Strengthen doctrine to guide the national response.* Incidents that begin with a single response discipline within one jurisdiction may quickly expand to multi-disciplinary, multi-jurisdictional incidents that require additional resources and capabilities. In order to ensure high-level organization and efficiency among multiple actors in these challenging and complex environments, the response community must rely on fundamental principles that guide the full range of response activities. NIMS forms the backbone of this doctrine and includes, among other things, an Incident Command System as the overall management structure for responding to an incident as well as the concept of Unified Command, which provides for and enables joint decisions and action based on mutually agreed-upon objectives, priorities, and plans among all homeland partners involved in the response effort without affecting individual agency authority, responsibility, or accountability. We will continue to expand and refine the full set of fundamental doctrinal principles underlying our National Response Framework. For example, we will incorporate and further emphasize the concept of readiness to act that is imperative for no-notice incidents as well as incidents that have the potential to expand rapidly in size, scope, or complexity. Through the framework, we will encourage engaged partnerships in which all organizations establish shared objectives, assess their capabilities, identify gaps, and work collaboratively to fill those gaps well in advance of an incident. We also

Roles and Responsibilities

In today's dynamic threat environment, we must strive for a national response based on engaged partnerships at and across all levels that enable us to anticipate where we should increase or reduce support based on changing circumstances. Success starts with understanding the following fundamental roles:

Community Response. *One of the fundamental response principles is that all incidents should be handled at the lowest jurisdictional level possible.* The initial response to the majority of incidents typically is handled by local responders within a single jurisdiction and goes no further. When incidents exceed available resources, the local or Tribal government may rely on mutual aid agreements with nearby localities or request additional support from the State. It is worth noting that for certain types of Federal assistance, Tribal nations work with the State, but, as sovereign entities, they can elect to deal directly with the Federal Government for other types of assistance.

State Response. *State governments have the primary responsibility for assisting local governments to respond to and recover from disasters and emergencies.* When an incident expands to challenge the resources and capabilities of the State coordinate requests for additional support, the State may request support from the private and nonprofit sector, turn to other States for support through the Emergency Management Assistance Compact, or call upon the Federal Government for assistance. States also may collaborate with one another to ensure a broader, more effective regional response.

Federal Response. *The Federal Government maintains a wide array of capabilities and resources that may be made available to States and local governments.* Federal assistance is provided when needed to support State and local efforts or lessen or avert the threat of a catastrophe within the United States. Accordingly, Federal response efforts are designed to complement and supplement, rather than supplant, the State and local response. The Federal Government also maintains relationships with private and non-profit sector entities to aid in facilitating additional support.

Private and Non-Profit Sector. *The private and non-profit sectors fulfill key roles and work closely with communities, States, and the Federal Government.* The private sector plays an essential role implementing plans for the rapid restoration of commercial activities and critical infrastructure operations, which can help mitigate consequences, improve quality of life, and accelerate recovery for communities and the Nation. Non-profit organizations serve a vital role by performing essential services within communities in times of need, such as mass sheltering, emergency food supplies, counseling services, or other vital support services.

Special Circumstances. *There are special circumstances where the Federal Government exercises a larger, more proactive role.* This includes catastrophic incidents when local and State governments require significant support, and incidents where Federal interests are directly implicated, such as those involving primary Federal jurisdiction or authorities. For example, the Federal Government will lead response efforts to render safe weapons of mass destruction and coordinate related activities with State and local partners, as appropriate.

will underscore that our national response must be scalable, flexible, and adaptable to respond to the full range of potential incidents that our Nation could confront.

- *Develop and apply joint planning and training processes.* An effective, coordinated response begins with sound planning well before an incident occurs. The planning process will translate policy, strategy, doctrine, and capabilities into specific tasks and courses of action to be undertaken during a response. The resulting plans must represent collaborative efforts involving communities, States, and the Federal Government as well as private sector and non-profit partners to ensure we effectively bring to bear all instruments of national power in our response to an incident. The planning effort also must be based on a clear set of planning assumptions and guided by a full range of national planning scenarios, depicting a spectrum of catastrophic man-made and natural disasters that would test our Nation's response capabilities. Finally, because each incident is unique, our planning processes must be dynamic and flexible, ensuring we have the ability not only to produce deliberate plans but also the ability to adapt our plans at the operational and tactical levels in a compressed period of time to address the specific characteristics of each incident.

Complementing our process for joint planning is a joint training and exercise program that will help response professionals practice the application of those plans well in advance of an actual incident. Ultimately, a continuous cycle of joint training and exercises will ensure that all government, private sector, and non-profit stakeholders are capable of fulfilling their roles and responsibilities and can achieve unity of effort when responding to a real-world natural or man-made disaster. It is vital that best practices and lessons learned from exercises be applied to continually improve our Nation's response.

- *Conduct advance readiness activities.* There are times when we are able to anticipate impending or emergent events that will require a national response, such as an upcoming hurricane season, a potential pandemic, or a period of heightened terrorist threat. We must capitalize on this critical window of opportunity to increase readiness activities. For example, we can pre-identify needs and fill gaps in our current capabilities or resources that will be required to address the specific nature of the forthcoming incident. We also will pre-position commodities such as water, ice, emergency meals, tarps, and other disaster supplies so they will be readily available for use. Additional advance readiness activities include establishing contracts with the private sector prior to an incident and developing pre-negotiated agreements with Federal departments and agencies to ensure that appropriate Federal resources are available during a crisis.

ASSESS SITUATION AND TAKE INITIAL ACTION

When an incident occurs, responders work to assess the situation – including possible causes, extent of affected population and geographic area, and the degree of damage – in order to take the initial actions that will save lives, mitigate suffering, and protect property. Our Nation must acknowledge the critical role of first responders to rapidly assess ongoing and emerging incidents. This includes effectively prioritizing and coordinating initial actions, mobilizing and deploying resources and capabilities, and anticipating additional support that may be needed.

> ### Situational Awareness
>
> Maintaining situational awareness is essential to assessing emerging incidents as well as conducting operations and ultimately ensuring the effective management of incident response. It demands that we prioritize information and develop a common operating picture, both of which require a well-developed national information management system and effective multi-agency coordination centers to support decision-making during incidents. The concept of situational awareness, along with other fundamental principles of incident management, is detailed in the chapter titled "Ensuring Long-Term Success."

- *Prioritize and coordinate initial actions to mitigate consequences.* Since there will be a degree of confusion and turmoil in the initial hours of an incident, it is critical that our Nation use standardized incident response structures and procedures to prioritize and coordinate initial actions. Our framework must better integrate the National Incident Management System (NIMS), which enables a consistent approach and allows multiple organizations to work together effectively. For example, as first responders arrive at the affected area, they must quickly establish on-scene incident command to coordinate the activities of numerous responders under a single structure. Using NIMS, the incident command develops an Incident Action Plan, which outlines incident priorities, objectives, and initial actions and drives the development of supporting plans. These initial activities may include search and rescue, evacuations, communication of key information to the public, restoration of essential critical infrastructure, and provision of community law enforcement, fire, and emergency medical services, among others. As the incident unfolds, the incident command will revise plans and courses of action based on changing circumstances.

- *Effectively mobilize and deploy people, resources, and capabilities.* In response, every minute counts, and a failure to quickly surge people, resources, and capabilities can result in lives lost, increased property damage, and cascading consequences that can magnify the effects of the incident. To ensure rapid mobilization and deployment of response assets, our National Response Framework must describe how this process occurs across various levels

---

Examples of Federal Field Teams

Since September 11, the Federal Government has strengthened deployable teams to help respond to natural and man-made disasters. These teams support the emergent needs of State, local, and Tribal jurisdictions or exercise Federal statutory responsibilities by providing specialized expertise and capabilities, establishing emergency response facilities, and supporting overall incident management.

- Emergency Response Teams (ERT) – to be replaced by the Federal Incident Response Support Teams (FIRST) and Incident Management Assistance Teams (IMAT)

- Damage Assessment Teams

- Nuclear Incident Response Team (NIRT)

- Disaster Medical Assistance Teams (DMATs)

- Department of Health and Human Services' Incident Response Coordination Team – formerly the Secretary's Emergency Response Team

- Department of Labor/Occupational Safety and Health Administration's Specialized Response Teams

- National Veterinary Response Teams (NVRT) – formerly the Veterinarian Medical Assistance Teams (VMATs)

- Disaster Mortuary Operational Response Teams (DMORTs)

- Medical Emergency Radiological Response Team (MERRT)

- National Medical Response Teams (NMRTs)

- Scientific and Technical Advisory and Response Teams (STARTs)

- Donations Coordination Teams

- Urban Search and Rescue (US&R) Task Forces

- Incident Management Teams (IMTs)

- Domestic Emergency Support Team (DEST)

- Domestic Animal and Wildlife Emergency Response Teams and Mitigation Assessment Team

of government and with the private and nonprofit sectors. In addition, all responders should be encouraged to maintain and regularly exercise notification systems and activation protocols. Activation and deployment should be a deliberate and informed – yet rapid – process that reflects the size, scope, nature, and complexity of an incident.

- *Anticipate additional support that may be needed.* Minute by minute, the scope and scale of an incident can rapidly evolve, such as when a hurricane changes course or it becomes apparent that a terrorist bombing is actually one in a series of attacks in multiple cities. Responders at all levels must be able to anticipate the course of an incident and associated requirements and work with their counterparts to surge or deescalate resources and capabilities as needed. While there is no substitute for experience, our National Response Framework must help drive joint planning and training programs that will help responders across all levels better anticipate alternative courses of action and work together effectively.

EXPAND OPERATIONAL CAPABILITIES, AS NEEDED

While the vast majority of incidents are effectively handled at the community level, some require additional support from nearby jurisdictions or the State, including through mutual aid agreements with other States. If needed, the Federal Government also will provide support. In catastrophic or highly complex events, all who respond should provide assistance in an organized fashion within the existing response framework, anticipating needs and coordinating with their partners in advance as opposed to waiting to be asked. As the incident grows in severity and complexity, our national response operations must effectively coordinate requests for additional support and integrate resources and capabilities into ongoing operations. It is critical that our Nation continue to improve and clearly describe the processes used to coordinate requests for additional support and integrate resources and capabilities into ongoing operations.

- *Effectively coordinate requests for additional support.* If resources and capabilities beyond the immediate area are required, the on-scene incident command requests additional support, activating response structures and personnel to support and coordinate the overall response. In many cases, resources and capabilities are provided from surrounding areas. Our Nation must work together to clarify the processes to request and provide assistance and ensure we have the necessary awareness, training, and familiarization programs for responders to execute related plans and agreements. This includes familiarization with the processes that States use to request support through mutual aid agreements as well as from the Federal Government and how the Federal Government provides this support to States. Effective support requires that all organizations review and update their existing agreements and plans, meet with their partners, and verify their expectations and capabilities on a regular basis.

- *Integrate resources and capabilities.* During large-scale incidents, we establish response structures and facilities to effectively receive, stage, track, and integrate incoming resources and capabilities into ongoing operations. For example, personnel are deployed to staging areas to receive commodities that can then be integrated into operations in support of the State and then distributed to communities. For large, complex incidents, resources and capabilities might arrive from a diverse array of organizations – ranging from multiple private-sector companies to non-governmental organizations to the Federal Government – through pre-arranged agreements and contracts. In order to assist with the full assimilation of resources and assets, we will continue to develop comprehensive and integrated logistics systems and procedures that enhance our Nation's overall response capabilities. In addition, our National Response Framework must describe the policies and procedures for how to manage disaster assistance offered by our international partners, as well as clarify responsibilities and procedures for inquiries regarding affected foreign nationals.

COMMENCE SHORT-TERM RECOVERY ACTIONS TO STABILIZE THE AFFECTED AREA AND DEMOBILIZE ASSETS

Even as the immediate imperatives for response to an incident are being addressed, the need to begin recovery operations emerges. In an almost imperceptible evolution, response efforts will transition to short-term recovery operations, such as the restoration of interrupted utility services, reestablishment of transportation routes, and the provision of food and shelter for those displaced by the disaster – actions that will help individuals, communities, and the Nation return to a general state of normalcy. While short-term recovery efforts are the primary responsibility of States and communities, they also involve significant contributions from all sectors of our society – Federal, State, local, and Tribal governments, the private sector, nonprofit partners, as well as individual citizens. As the priorities and needs of an incident evolve, people, assets, and resources will be reassigned or demobilized to provide a flexible and scalable response, evolving as needs evolve, changing as the incident priorities change. As immediate life-saving and life-sustaining activities subside, and short-term recovery decisions are made over a period of weeks or even months, we must recognize that these efforts are steps to an effective transition to long-term rebuilding and revitalization efforts.

ENSURE AN EFFECTIVE TRANSITION TO LONG-TERM REBUILDING AND REVITALIZATION EFFORTS

Ensuring a successful transition from short-term recovery to rebuilding and revitalization efforts is vital and must include active participation and leadership by the breadth of political, economic, private, and non-profit actors that form the fiber of any community. Rebuilding and revitalization efforts are distinguished from shorter-term recovery efforts not only by the length of time involved, but also by the scope and nature of the incident, the complexity of efforts required to regenerate infrastructure, and the effect on the social fabric of the community and region.

Rebuilding and revitalizing those communities so devastated or severely affected by a catastrophic incident that a State or region is overwhelmed can take several months and sometimes years, depending on the severity and extent of destruction. Some cases might require the complete reconstruction of critical infrastructure and key resources, redevelopment of homes and long-term housing solutions, and the restoration of economic growth and vitality.

In the past, we have undertaken reconstruction operations for major catastrophes in an *ad hoc* and reactive fashion, developing large-scale disaster-specific rebuilding approaches and tools only after major crises arise. The resulting process of rebuilding has been slow, complex, and extremely expensive. Notwithstanding the tremendous efforts of the individuals involved, the challenges of an *ad hoc* approach are reflected in the experiences in lower Manhattan after the September 11 attacks, in the southeastern United States during the 2004 hurricane season that witnessed landfall of four major hurricanes within six weeks, and in the Gulf Coast region after Hurricane Katrina.

Going forward, we must develop a comprehensive – but not bureaucratic or government-centric – framework wherein communities that are directly or indirectly affected by a large-scale disaster can flourish on a sustainable path to rebuilding and revitalization. This framework and accompanying plans must be closely guided by, and have at their core, the citizens, private sector, and faith-based and community organizations that are most severely and directly affected. After all, individual citizens and the private and non-profit sectors are our society's wells of creativity, innovation, and resourcefulness, and they have the greatest stake in, and urgency for, revitalizing their community.

The majority of reconstruction efforts will occur beyond the Federal Government's purview. However, the Federal Government, in collaboration with all stakeholders, will draw upon and apply the field's most innovative thinking, lessons learned, and best practices to create a comprehensive framework for our Nation that fully appreciates free markets and the vast power of incentives and empowers individuals, businesses, and non-profit groups in the decisions about the future of their communities.

In order to develop this new framework, our Nation must continue to assess the challenges in this area and provide recommendations to improve our ability to rebuild and revitalize areas following a catastrophic natural or man-made disaster. We must determine how Federal, State, local, and Tribal governments, the private and non-profit sectors, and communities can improve collaboration and develop recommendations that further economic renewal and help stabilize and reconstruct communities.

In addressing these challenges, Federal, State, local, and Tribal governments, the private and nonprofit sectors, and communities must be focused on citizens – and not on bureaucracy or processes – and be guided by the concepts of compassion, speed, efficiency, common sense, and the devolution of as many decisions as reasonably possible to individual citizens, businesses, and communities. Specific areas of focus include:

- *Restore community services and the economy.* In the wake of a catastrophic event, all facets of society will need to work together to restore communities and the economy. This includes helping to facilitate the return of private, non-profit, and government operations to the affected area. Individuals, communities, and private sector and non-profit entities should strive to resume their services as quickly as possible, while government at all levels should carry out activities and investments that foster this rapid and orderly revitalization. Federal, State, local, and Tribal governments may consider a range of actions based on the circumstances and careful consideration of the situation and, in some cases, may temporarily reduce or waive regulations that could result in unintended consequences from large-scale incidents.

- *Organize planning efforts among key players.* The Nation should coalesce around public-private partnerships that can more effectively integrate and coordinate collective recovery efforts. This requires plans and policies that support basic needs such as housing, medical care, and the food service industry. In some circumstances, this will require the creation of special purpose entities and unique, temporary tax or other financial incentives that foster cooperation and collective engagement in rebuilding of the affected communities. In addition, as warranted and in accordance with existing laws and regulations, the Federal Government can scale back select requirements that communities match Federal expenditures with certain percentage of funding from their own budgets.

- *Facilitate long-term assistance for displaced victims.* Ensuring the availability of medium-term housing and promotion of long-term housing solutions for the affected area are often important initial measures. Other focus areas must include care and treatment of affected persons in terms of sustained medical care and additional measures for social, political, environmental, and economic restoration. In order to be effective, long-term efforts to assist displaced victims must begin as soon as possible following response efforts, in conjunction with short-term recovery.

- *Rebuild critical infrastructure.* A key Federal role in long-term reconstruction involves both rebuilding the most essential critical infrastructure and providing economic incentives, when appropriate, to support the return of citizens and the private sector to the affected community. Because this is a very different problem from response and immediate recovery efforts, long-term rebuilding and revitalization must be addressed through tailored approaches that creatively engage the full spectrum of government, private sector, and non-profit entities. Furthermore, including mitigation measures in critical infrastructure designs during the restoration process also is important for reducing the consequences of future similar events.

Ensuring Long-Term Success

Preventing and disrupting terrorist attacks; protecting the American people, critical infrastructure, and key resources; and responding to and recovering from those incidents that do occur are enduring homeland security responsibilities. In order to help fulfill those responsibilities over the long term, we will continue to strengthen the principles, systems, structures, and institutions that cut across the homeland security enterprise and support our activities to secure the Homeland. Ultimately, this will help ensure the success of our *Strategy* to secure the Nation.

Risk Management

The assessment and management of risk underlies the full spectrum of our homeland security activities, including decisions about when, where, and how to invest in resources that eliminate, control, or mitigate risks. In the face of multiple and diverse catastrophic possibilities, we accept that risk – a function of threats, vulnerabilities, and consequences – is a permanent condition. We must apply a risk-based framework across all homeland security efforts in order to identify and assess potential hazards (including their downstream effects), determine what levels of relative risk are acceptable, and prioritize and allocate resources among all homeland security partners, both public and private, to prevent, protect against, and respond to and recover from all manner of incidents. A disciplined approach to managing risk will help to achieve overall effectiveness and efficiency in securing the Homeland. In order to develop this discipline, we as a Nation must organize and help mature the profession of risk management by adopting common risk analysis principles and standards, as well as a professional lexicon.

Culture of Preparedness

Our entire Nation shares common responsibilities in homeland security. In order to help prepare the Nation to carry out these responsibilities, we will continue to foster a Culture of Preparedness that permeates all levels of our society – from individual citizens, businesses, and non-profit organizations to Federal, State, local, and Tribal government officials and authorities. This Culture rests on four principles.

The first principle of our Culture of Preparedness is a shared acknowledgement that creating a prepared Nation will be an enduring challenge. As individual citizens we must guard against complacency, and as a society we must balance the sense of optimism that is fundamental to the American character with a sober recognition that future catastrophes will occur. The certainty of future calamities should inform and motivate our preparedness, and we will continue to emphasize the responsibility of the entire Nation to be flexible and ready to cope with a broad range of challenges.

The second principle is the importance of individual and collective initiative to counter fundamental biases toward reactive responses and approaches. Our Culture, therefore, must encourage and reward innovation and new ways of thinking as well as better align authority and responsibility so that those who are responsible for a mission or task have the authority to act.

The third principle is that individual citizens, communities, the private sector, and non-profit organizations each perform a central role in homeland security. Citizen and community preparedness are among the most effective means of securing the Homeland, and leadership must continue at all levels to promote and strengthen their preparedness, including through public dialogue and specialized programs such as the "Ready" campaign, the Nation's public service initiative for individual and corporate preparedness (see ready.gov for more information). All Americans must share in the full range of homeland security activities, including prevention and protection, but it is particularly important that we all take responsibility for increasing the likelihood that we can survive an incident and care for our own basic needs in the immediate aftermath. As more Americans contribute to homeland security through self-reliance and mutual assistance, we reduce the burden on our emergency responders so they can focus on those most in need.

We also will continue to encourage the preparedness of other homeland security stakeholders, including private sector and non-profit groups such as non-governmental organizations and faith-based groups and, whenever appropriate, incorporate them as full partners into our national preparedness efforts across all homeland security disciplines. The private sector is particularly important in this endeavor. As highlighted throughout this *Strategy*, the private sector is the Nation's primary provider of goods and services and the owner and operator of approximately 85 percent of our critical infrastructure. It is an essential partner in ensuring structural and operational resilience that protects the American people, establishing supply chain security to help deny terrorist weapons and material entry into the Homeland, and reporting suspicious activities at work sites that could uncover and ultimately help disrupt terrorist activity. The private sector also is a critical partner in rebuilding communities devastated or severely affected by a catastrophic incident as well as in fielding scientific and technological advancements that can help secure the Homeland. Due to the multiple and essential roles the private sector plays across all areas of homeland security, continued collaboration and engagement with the private sector to strengthen preparedness is imperative.

The fourth principle of our Culture of Preparedness is the responsibility of each level of government in fostering a prepared Nation. Although Federal, State, local, and Tribal governments will have roles and responsibilities unique to each, our Culture must continue to embrace the notion of partnership among all levels of government. Built upon a foundation of partnerships, common goals, and shared responsibility, the creation of our Culture of Preparedness is an enduring touchstone for homeland security.

HOMELAND SECURITY MANAGEMENT SYSTEM

In order to continue strengthening the foundations of a prepared Nation, we will establish and institutionalize a comprehensive Homeland Security Management System that incorporates all stakeholders. Relevant departments and agencies of the Federal Government must take the lead in implementing this system, and State, local, and Tribal governments are highly encouraged to ultimately adopt fully compatible and complementary processes and practices as part of a full-scale national effort.

Our current approach to managing homeland security has focused on doctrine and planning through the National Preparedness Guidelines (NPG). Called for in Homeland Security Presidential Directive-8, issued on December 17, 2003, the NPG delineates readiness targets, priorities, standards for preparedness assessments and strategies, and a system for assessing the Nation's overall level of preparedness to prevent, protect against, and respond to and recover from incidents. The NPG aligns national efforts by using national planning scenarios that represent a wide range of catastrophic terrorist attacks and natural disasters that would stretch the Nation's prevention, protection, and response capabilities. Those scenarios form the basis of the 37 essential capabilities, identified in the NPG and the accompanying Target Capabilities List, that must be developed or maintained, in whole or in part, by various levels of government across our homeland security efforts. In this manner, the NPG constitutes a capabilities-based preparedness process for making informed decisions about managing homeland risk and prioritizing homeland security investments across disciplines, jurisdictions, regions, and levels of government, helping us to answer how prepared we are, how prepared we need to be, and how we prioritize efforts to close the gap.

We must build on this current process in order to establish a more deliberate and comprehensive system that will ensure unity of effort and help maximize success as we work to prevent and disrupt terrorism, protect the American people, critical infrastructure and key resources, and respond to and recover from incidents that do occur. This new Homeland Security Management System (depicted in Figure 1) will involve a continuous, mutually reinforcing cycle of activity across four phases.

- **Phase One: Guidance.** The first phase in our Homeland Security Management System encompasses overarching homeland security guidance. It is the foundation of our system, and it must be grounded in clearly articulated and up-to-date homeland and relevant national security policies, with coordinated supporting strategies, doctrine, and planning guidance flowing from and fully synchronizing with these policies. Accordingly, we will update, clarify, and consolidate, where necessary, homeland and national security presidential directives and other key policies, all of which encompass high-level executive articulations of the broad homeland security goals we must achieve.

- **Phase Two: Planning.** The second phase is a deliberate and dynamic system that translates our policies, strategies, doctrine, and planning guidance into a family of strategic, operational, and tactical plans. These plans should be coordinated with relevant stakeholders, consistent with the fundamental roles and responsibilities of local, Tribal, State, and Federal governments bring to bear all appropriate instruments of national power and influence, assign activities to specific homeland security actors, and appropriately sequence these activities against a timeline for implementation.

    Strategic plans educate and drive resource requirements and capabilities, laying the foundation for more detailed operational and tactical plans. Based on the resource and capability requirements identified in strategic plans, operational and tactical plans prescribe the actions of all applicable stakeholders arranged in time and space in order to achieve specific goals. For the Homeland Security Management System to be effective and address long-range challenges across multiple disciplines, all homeland security partners should develop a planning capability that may also be employed during times of crisis.

Figure 1
HOMELAND SECURITY MANAGEMENT SYSTEM

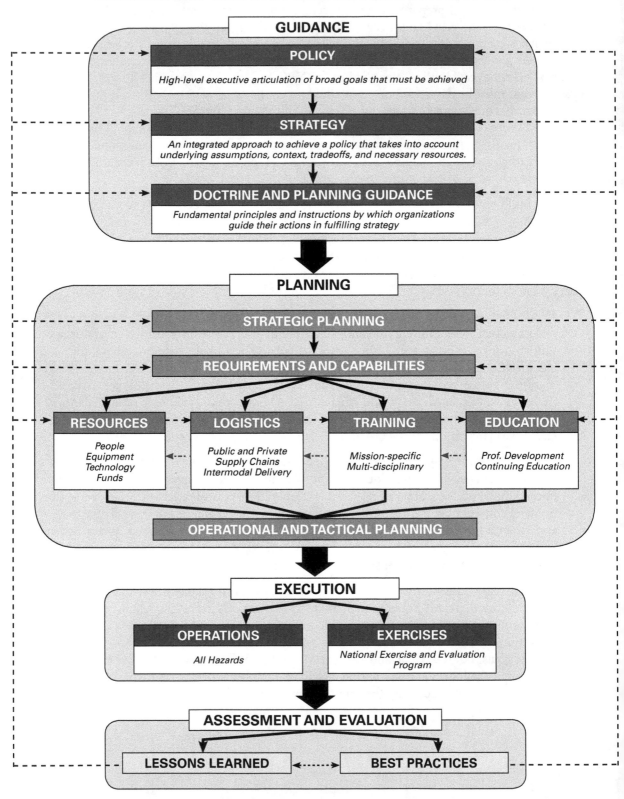

Requirements and capabilities within the planning phase of our system also must place particular emphasis on training and education so that homeland security professionals not only acquire the specific functional skills that are needed to successfully execute operational plans but also understand the broader strategic context in which these plans will be executed. Leadership development must be emphasized in this education and training process, because planning and execution across a wide array of communities, organizational structures, and professions requires specific leadership skills. The second phase ultimately culminates in tactical plans by homeland security partners that describe the specific field-level activities they will undertake to fulfill the responsibilities assigned to them in the operational plan.

- *Phase Three: Execution.* The third phase in the Homeland Security Management System encompasses the execution of operational and tactical-level plans. This may occur as actual operations in response to real-world events or may happen as part of an exercise, including through the National Exercise Program, that allows us to practice the plan and ensure all actors fully understand their roles and responsibilities.

> **Investing in Intellectual and Human Capital**
>
> In order to ensure the success of the Homeland Security Management System, our Nation must further develop a community of homeland security professionals. This requires establishing multidisciplinary education in homeland and relevant national security policies and strategies; the planning process; execution of operations and exercises; and overall assessment and evaluation. Furthermore, this should include an understanding and appreciation of appropriate regions, religions, cultures, legal systems, and languages. Education must continue outside the classroom as well – in order to enhance knowledge and learning, build trust and familiarity among diverse homeland security practitioners, break down organizational stovepipes, and advance the exchange of ideas and best practices, we must continue to develop interagency and intergovernmental assignments and fellowship opportunities, tying them to promotions and professional advancement. Executive Order 13434 of May 17, 2007 ("National Security Professional Development") and the resulting *National Strategy for the Development of Security Professionals* are essential steps forward in meeting these educational needs, and we will continue to build on these endeavors to ensure that we have the necessary depth and breadth of intellectual and human capital across all levels of homeland security partnerships and disciplines.

- *Phase Four: Assessment and Evaluation.* The fourth phase involves the continual assessment and evaluation of both operations and exercises. This phase of the system will produce lessons learned and best practices that must be incorporated back into all phases of the Homeland Security Management System. This sequence of activities ensures our highly adaptive system reflects current realities and remains responsive to a dynamic, changing homeland security environment.

Because homeland security is a shared responsibility, the Federal Government must provide leadership and guidance for non-Federal partners across the four phases of the Homeland Security Management System. For the Homeland Security Management System to succeed, Federal dollars must be allocated based on constantly improving risk assessments and on accountability for results; once allocated, funds must be used to support or develop operational plans and their derivative requirements and capabilities. In addition, our Nation still faces the challenge of developing tools for assessing our overall security posture and measuring the effectiveness of Federal assistance. We therefore must develop assessment tools that measure not only State, local, and Tribal response capabilities but also capabilities in support of our prevention and protection goals. These tools must recognize and reward partnership with and among neighboring jurisdictions and regions and all levels of government.

INCIDENT MANAGEMENT

While our Homeland Security Management System provides a framework for integrating four essential phases in a deliberate process to secure the Homeland, there will be times when incidents force the homeland security community to compress this cycle of activity and assume a more crisis-oriented posture. Decision-making during crises and periods of heightened concern, however, is different from decision-making during a steady-state of activity, and we must develop a comprehensive approach that will help Federal, State, local, and Tribal authorities manage incidents across all homeland security efforts.

Our approach will build upon the current National Incident Management System (NIMS). An outgrowth of Homeland Security Presidential Directive-5 (HSPD-5), issued on February 28, 2003, NIMS focuses largely on stakeholders in the discipline of response. Incidents, however, are not limited to natural and man-made disasters that strike the Homeland. They also include, for example, threats developing overseas, law enforcement and public health actions and investigations, and even specific protective measures taken at critical infrastructure sites, for example. In order to realize the full intent of HSPD-5, our new approach to incident management must apply not only to response and recovery but also to the prevention and protection phases of an incident as well. Federal efforts must be directed toward coordination of resources across sectors (public, private, and non-profit), disciplines, and among Federal, State, local, and Tribal officials.

Incident management rests on a core set of common principles and requirements. The first of these is an Incident Command System, which provides the overall structure for managing an incident. Our current system for incident command has five major functional areas: command, operations, planning, logistics, and finance and administration. Although a sixth area – intelligence – is currently applied on an *ad hoc* basis, we must institutionalize this area throughout our new approach in support of prevention and protection activities. Unified Command is a second core principle. The Federal Government must fully adopt and implement this principle, which is commonly used at the State and local levels and provides the basis from which multiple agencies can work together effectively to manage an incident

> **Principles and Requirements of Incident Management**
>
> Incident Command System
>
> Unified Command
>
> Crisis Action Planning Resources
>
> Situational Awareness
>
> Prioritization of Information
>
> Multi-Agency Coordination Centers
>
> Skilled Leaders and Partners
>
> Training and Exercises

by ensuring that all decisions will be based upon mutually agreed upon objectives and plans, regardless of the number of entities or jurisdictions involved.

Crisis action planning is a third key principle in our approach to incident management. This planning process takes existing contingency plans and procedures and rapidly adapts them to address the requirements of the current crisis or event of concern in a compressed timeframe. We must ensure that all stakeholders across all homeland security disciplines have the ability to transition quickly from contingency planning to crisis action planning. They also must be able to provide resources – a fourth requirement – in support of their plans and activities, and we call on all stakeholders to have predetermined capabilities available on a short deployment timeline.

The maintenance of situational awareness through timely and accurate information is a fifth core principle integral to incident management. It requires continuous sharing, monitoring, verification, and synthesis of information to support informed decisions on how to best manage threats, potential threats, disasters, or events of concern. In order to help facilitate situational awareness and decision-making, we must prioritize incident information – a sixth requirement. While timely information is valuable, it also can be overwhelming. We must be able to identify what is required to assist decision makers and then rapidly summarize and prioritize the information we receive from multiple reporting systems. In order to be successful, our new approach to incident management also must have an information management system that integrates key information and defines national information requirements.

A seventh requirement of incident management consists of the various multi-agency coordination centers that exist throughout all levels of government. They are essential to maintaining situa-

> ### Interoperable and Resilient Communications
>
> Our Nation continues to confront two distinct communications challenges: interoperability and survivability. Unimpeded and timely flow of information in varying degrees across multiple operational systems and between different disciplines and jurisdictions is critical to command, control, and coordination of operational activities. To achieve interoperability, we must have compatible equipment, standard operating procedures, planning, mature governance structures, and a collaborative culture that enables all necessary parties to work together seamlessly. Survivable communications infrastructure is even more fundamental. To achieve survivability, our national security and emergency preparedness communications systems must be resilient – either able to withstand destructive forces regardless of cause or sufficiently redundant to suffer damage and remain reliable. Without the appropriate application of interoperable communications technologies, standards, and governance structures, effective and safe incident management will be hindered. Although much progress has been made, effective communication during major disasters requiring multi-jurisdictional coordination depends on continued improvement to our Nation's communications systems.

tional awareness and overall incident management, and they assist in the flow of information, the reporting of actions and activities, and ultimately the development of a common operating picture, but they also are hubs for coordinating operational activities during an incident. Examples include State, local, and Tribal emergency operations centers; State, local, and Tribal fusion centers; the National Operations Center, National Infrastructure Coordination Center, and the Federal Emergency Management Agency's National Response Coordination Center (all part of the Department of Homeland Security); the Federal Bureau of Investigation's Strategic Information and Operations Center and National Joint Terrorist Task Force (both part of the Department of Justice); and the National Counterterrorism Center (part of the Office of the Director of National Intelligence). We will continue to develop and strengthen these centers and systems to ensure that activities are better coordinated and related information is shared among multiple agencies.

People exist at the heart of our refocused incident management approach, and deploying people with the skills necessary to manage each incident is the eighth key principle. Building on the professional development initiatives that are part of our Homeland Security Management System, we will ensure that the most qualified professionals are identified in advance so that they may be quickly and efficiently activated and deployed during an incident. We will embrace and institute a continuous training cycle to ensure that leaders and partners at all levels of government are fully trained and well versed in the principles of incident management. Finally, we will conduct exercises, consistent with the National Exercise Program, so that all stakeholders can ensure they are fully capable of executing their incident management responsibilities.

SCIENCE AND TECHNOLOGY

The United States derives much of its strength from its advantage in the realm of science and technology (S&T), and we must continue to use this advantage and encourage innovative research and development to assist in protecting and defending against the range of natural and man-made threats confronting the Homeland.

Over the past six years, focused partnerships with our Nation's vast and varied research enterprise, which includes businesses, research institutes, universities, government laboratories as well as Federal departments and agencies, have yielded significant capabilities that are helping us to better protect the lives and livelihoods of the American people. For instance, the focused application of the Nation's nuclear expertise has produced improved tools for countering the threat of nuclear terrorism against the Homeland. We also have applied biometric technologies and systems to enhance the security of travel documents and inhibit the movement of terrorists internationally and across our borders. The development and application of a variety of chemical, biological, radiological, and nuclear countermeasures are helping to prevent WMD terrorism and address the public health consequences that can stem from a range of natural and man-made disasters. We also have upgraded the technical capabilities of our first responders through the provision of decontamination equipment and protective gear; these advances serve not only to better protect our Nation's first responders but also to increase their ability to save the lives of others. Other improvements in the critical area of S&T include additional funding of independent analysis for homeland security S&T research and setting of standards for homeland security technology.

We will continue to build upon this foundation of scientific and technological advancement and support funding for research and development to further strengthen the security of the Homeland. We will streamline processes and reduce red tape in order to enhance our partnerships with the country's national research enterprise, including within and among Federal departments and agencies. Specifically, we will continue to engage in disciplined dialogue about the threats we face, our strategies to counter them, and how S&T can bridge gaps in approaches or facilitate the more effective and efficient achievement of our objectives. Our collaborative S&T efforts should continue to explore existing or emerging technologies used for multiple or non-security specific purposes and develop rapid prototyping methods to adapt them to fill critical homeland security needs. Research in systems and operations science that will allow the integration of technology into functional capability is of equal importance. For example, a sound scientific knowledge base regarding health and medical response systems could improve our ability to manage the health consequences of disasters. By promoting the evolution of current technologies and fielding new, revolutionary capabilities, S&T will remain an essential and enduring enabler of our *Strategy*.

LEVERAGING INSTRUMENTS OF NATIONAL POWER AND INFLUENCE

In the wake of both the September 11 terrorist attacks and lessons learned from our response to Hurricane Katrina, the United States has used its instruments of national power and influence – diplomatic, information, military, economic, financial, intelligence, and law enforcement – to prevent terrorism, protect the lives and livelihoods of the American people, and respond to and recover from incidents. For instance, we have enhanced our ability to analyze and integrate all intelligence pertaining to terrorism through the establishment of the Office of the Director of National Intelligence and the National Counterterrorism Center as well as the creation of an Information Sharing Environment. The general sharing of information, however, extends beyond terror-related intelligence, and we will continue to enhance our processes for sharing all relevant and appropriate information throughout our levels of government and with the private and non-profit sectors and our foreign partners on the full range of homeland security issues.

We are applying targeted financial sanctions to identify and isolate terrorist financiers and facilitators and using a restructured approach to economic assistance, both overseas to meet current and long-term challenges such as ter-

> **Information Sharing Environment**
>
> In December 2004, Congress passed and the President signed the Intelligence Reform and Terrorism Prevention Act of 2004 (IRTPA). IRTPA calls for, among other things, the creation of the Information Sharing Environment (ISE) – a trusted partnership among all levels of government, the private sector, and our foreign partners to detect, prevent, disrupt, preempt, and mitigate the effects of terrorism against the territory, people, and interests of the United States through the appropriate exchange of terrorism information.
>
> In addition, IRTPA establishes a Program Manager for the ISE who is responsible for overseeing its implementation. With the enactment of the Implementing Recommendations of the 9/11 Commission Act of 2007, the ISE has been expanded further to include not only "terrorism Information" as defined in IRTPA but also other categories of homeland security information and weapons of mass destruction information.

rorism, and here at home to assist in the recovery of communities severely affected by catastrophic homeland security incidents. We also are building enduring public-private partnerships to leverage our Nation's economic power by driving improvements in global security practices, including measures relating to international air travel and global supply chains. We are engaging in transformational diplomacy within the international arena as well as leveraging our engagement with and among Federal, State, local, Tribal, and private sector partners here in the Homeland. We will continue to utilize our public diplomacy and strategic communications resources to offer a positive vision of hope and opportunity that is rooted in our most basic values; work with our partners to isolate and discredit those who espouse ideologies of hate and oppression; and nurture common interests and values between Americans and peoples of different countries, cultures, and faiths across the world.

As we sustain the evolution underway in these areas, success in securing the Homeland requires that we prioritize the continued transformation of our law enforcement and military instruments of national power. Our Nation's law enforcement community – Federal, State, local, and Tribal authorities – collaborate to detect, prevent, and disrupt a range of threats to the public, including terrorism. Our Federal law enforcement community is composed of more than 100,000 full-time personnel who play a decisive leadership role with respect to terrorism and related homeland security matters, including collecting and analyzing significant terrorist and criminal information through more than 100 Federal Bureau of Investigation-led Joint Terrorism Task Forces. Moreover, the U.S. Attorney for each of our country's 94 Federal judicial districts leads an Anti-Terrorism Advisory Council that brings together a cross-section of investigators and prosecutors from all levels of government, as well as first responders and private security personnel, to coordinate counterterrorism initiatives and support the operational efforts of the Joint Terrorism Task Forces.

Our State, local, and Tribal law enforcement communities, representing more than one million personnel from coast to coast, also play an integral role in the all-hazards approach to homeland security. Their role includes active engagement in a broad array of activities that detect and investigate potential threats, protect the American people and critical infrastructures, and restore and maintain law and order in the wake of catastrophic incidents. We will continue to work with and enable State and local fusion centers to leverage their capabilities in the War on Terror and maximize the flow of information among Federal, State, local, and Tribal entities. State, local, and Tribal law enforcement and other first responders also are the leaders in maintaining public safety by performing other essential response services, such as conducting evacuations.

Given the significant overall demands of homeland security and the simultaneously increasing technological and organizational sophistication of terrorist and criminal elements, there is a growing need to better manage and more efficiently leverage all of our law enforcement resources. Specifically, we must build on six years of progress to further enhance collaboration among our numerous law enforcement entities, developing a common baseline for law enforcement activities (e.g., standardizing information collection and collation, reporting procedures, and data archiving across all jurisdictions in order to improve analysis and detection of emerging threats or patterns) so that they may work together seamlessly throughout the Nation. This common approach must be capable of tailoring activities at each level to support specific priorities of importance to their respective communities and, as necessary, be able to fulfill select requests for information as part of the broader national effort to secure the Homeland. The approach should be consciously designed to be all-crimes relevant so that investments in information technology, communications equipment, and other support structures are used to drive efficiencies across the full range of law enforcement activities. We also will continue to fund training and exercises as well as the development of a common baseline for reporting and requesting information requirements. By enabling seamless integration and true unity of effort among all Federal, State, local, and Tribal law enforcement entities, we will better protect and defend the Homeland and the American people.

Our Nation's armed forces are crucial partners in homeland security. Our active, reserve, and National Guard forces are integrated into communities throughout our country, and they bring to bear the largest and most diverse workforce and capabilities in government to protect the United States from direct attacks and conduct missions to deter, prevent, and defeat threats against our Nation.

Over the past several years, our armed forces have been preparing to meet a wider range of challenges to our Nation by restructuring their capabilities, rearranging their global force posture, and adapting forces to better fight the War on Terror. While defending the Homeland is appropriately a top priority for the Department of Defense, the country's active, reserve, and National Guard forces also must continue to enhance their ability to provide support to civil authorities, not only to help prevent terrorism but also to respond to and recover from man-made and natural disasters that do occur. Working with the Nation's Governors and State Adjutants General, the Department of Defense must develop operational plans based upon the national planning scenarios that will integrate and synchronize military forces to achieve unity of effort in support of homeland security missions across the Nation. These plans will determine specific military requirements and capabilities for accomplishing homeland security missions that will most effectively be met by the combined effort of active, reserve, and National Guard forces.

LEGISLATIVE BRANCH

Homeland security at the Federal level is not the sole purview of the executive branch of government. The Congress also must take bold steps to fulfill its responsibilities in the national effort to secure the Homeland and protect the American people. The current committee structure, for example, creates competing initiatives and requirements and fails to establish clear and consistent priorities or provide optimal oversight. Accordingly, both houses of the Congress should take action to further streamline the organization and structure of those committees that authorize and appropriate homeland security-related funds and otherwise oversee homeland security missions. The Congress also should fully embrace a risk-based funding approach so that we best prioritize our limited resources to meet our most critical homeland security goals and objectives first, as opposed to distributing funds and making decisions based on political considerations. In addition, Congress should help ensure that we have the necessary tools to address changing technologies and homeland security threats while protecting privacy and civil liberties. Finally, in the same manner that Congress was an important partner in building an effective national security system during the Cold War and beyond, a strong partnership with Congress will be essential to help secure the Homeland in the years ahead.

CONCLUSION

Since the turn of the millennium, our Nation has endured history's deadliest attack of international terrorism and the most destructive natural disaster to strike American soil. In the face of these challenges, America has responded courageously, with focus and clarity of purpose, and today we are safer, stronger, and better prepared to address the full range of catastrophic events, including man-made accidents and natural disasters, that threaten us. Our work, however, is far from over. We remain resolute in our commitment to prevent and disrupt terrorist attacks in the Homeland, protect the American people and the Nation's critical infrastructure and key resources, and effectively respond to and recover from those incidents that do occur. Working together, our Nation will secure the Homeland in order to sustain our way of life – now and for generations to come.

Printed in the USA
CPSIA information can be obtained
at www.ICGtesting.com
JSHW052020140824
68134JS00027B/2561